# GCSE Student Text

## Lorna Smith

# Seamus Heaney, Gillian Clarke
# & Pre-1914 Poetry

Series editor:
**Steve Eddy**

Philip Allan Updates
Market Place
Deddington
Oxfordshire
OX15 0SE
tel: 01869 338652
fax: 01869 337590
e-mail: sales@philipallan.co.uk
www.philipallan.co.uk

ISBN-13: 978–1–84489–229–7
ISBN-10: 1–84489–229–8

Printed by Raithby, Lawrence & Co Ltd, Leicester

**Environmental information**

The paper on which this title is printed is sourced from managed, sustainable forests.

# Contents

## Study and revision

## Context

## Poem by poem: Heaney

## Poem by poem: Clarke

# Poem by poem: Pre-1914 Poetry Bank

## Themes

## Style

## Comparing poems

# Tackling the exam

# Answers

# Glossary of literary terms

# Study and revision

This guide is intended for you to use throughout your GCSE English literature course. It will help you while you are studying the poems for the first time and later when you are revising. It explores in detail every poem in the AQA *Anthology* by Seamus Heaney and Gillian Clarke, as well as all the poems in the Pre-1914 Poetry Bank. It makes suggestions for comparing poems and cross-referencing between them. Enjoy using it, and good luck in the exam!

## How to approach poetry

> Prose; words in their best order; — poetry; the *best* words in the best order.
>
> (Coleridge, *Table Talk*, 27 April 1823)

> Poetry is the record of the best and happiest moments of the happiest and best minds.
>
> (Shelley, *A Defence of Poetry*, 1821)

Perhaps the most important thing to remember about reading poetry is that it was written to be enjoyed and to inspire — not to be studied for an examination. Try to read each poem in the spirit in which it was intended to be read. It wasn't meant as a puzzle to be cracked or something to catch you out.

When you come to a poem for the first time, it is best to read it carefully all the way through. Don't stop at any unfamiliar words or ideas — reading the whole thing should give a sense of the feel and mood of the poem. This will help when you go back over any tricky areas. Then reread it several more times. Ask yourself what it is about and what thoughts and ideas the poet may have wanted you to come away with.

Ideally, read it *aloud* to yourself. That way, you will be reading it at the pace the poet intended. You may hear sound effects that you would not have noticed if you had only read it in your head.

# How to make the most of this guide

## Context

This section of the book gives background information on the two modern poets and some key themes. You will not be tested on this, but it is useful to understand something about the poets and their backgrounds when you read their work. The timeline also provides useful information on the pre-1914 poets.

## Poem by poem

Before reading the notes and information on any poem, it is important that you read the poem again to yourself — preferably several times. You may have read it already in class, but even so it is a good idea to refresh your memory before studying it.

### Key point

Top tip: One trick is to use removable sticky notes. Write down key points about a particular poem and stick the labels next to the poem in the *Anthology*. You can move the labels around easily, then remove the notes when you don't need them any more.

As you use this guide, it will be helpful to take notes — you will remember much more if you *write down* key facts. However, *remember that you are not allowed to use annotated poems in the examination*. You are allowed to annotate your class copy, but you will be given a clean copy before the exam.

- For each person, first read through the 'Glossary' to check that you understand the less obvious words and phrases that it contains. Does this help you to understand a line that may have been puzzling you?
- The 'What happens?' paragraph is a brief summary of the 'story' of the poem and what it is about. It should give you an overview. There may be a 'Key point' box, which will give you extra information to help you understand the poem.
- The 'Structure', 'Language' and 'Imagery' sections should help you to explore the poem in more detail. Take your time over these. Look back at the poem to see each example in context and see if you can find more examples of the high-lighted features (such as rhyming couplets, alliteration or similes) so that you have plenty of evidence at your fingertips ready for the exam. If you are not familiar with the literary terms used, you can look them up in the 'Glossary of literary terms' at the end of this book.
- The 'Ideas to consider' section is one of the most important. It includes aspects that the poet wanted us to think carefully about— which is, perhaps, why they wrote the poem. You may simply be invited to share the poet's appreciation of a beautiful place, but often you will be drawn further. You might be encouraged to contemplate a new idea or to see something in a new light. What point is

the poet making? Is the poet successful in conveying his or her thoughts and attitudes? Where do your sympathies lie? Have your own thoughts and attitudes been influenced as a result? 'Pause for thought' boxes contain key questions. Read the questions carefully, considering the points they contain, and make your mind up. The answers will not be obvious and there is no clear right or wrong, so make sure that you can support your point of view using the text.

## Themes and style

When you have looked at all (or most of) the poems, read the sections of this book on 'Themes' and 'Style' carefully.

- 'Themes' looks at the poetry of Heaney and Clarke, identifying individual and shared themes. It gives you all you need to know about these modern poems in order to compare them to the pre-1914 texts.
- 'Style' contains information on viewpoint, setting and atmosphere, symbolism, imagery, rhythm, rhyme and metre, alliteration and assonance, and the poets' choice of language. It includes a table enabling you to compare the style of each modern poet with the pre-1914 poets.

## Comparing poems and tackling the exam

These final sections show you how to put everything together.

- 'Comparing poems' suggests how you can link poems by the same poet and by different poets. It includes a table of the main ways in which the poems might be compared and contrasted. It illustrates various ways in which you can plan essays, with some sample notes and paragraphs.
- 'Tackling the exam' gives hints on how to do as well as you can on the big day, with help on timing, planning your answer and choosing the right question for you. It includes handy opening phrases to use at various stages of your essay, along with some sample questions to practise with, and a sample A* answer.

# Weighing up the evidence

Having looked at what you should do, let's look at what you shouldn't do. There is no point in simply memorising chunks of this guide and regurgitating them in the examination, however secure this might make you feel.

Remember that the only way you are going to achieve good marks is to answer the question set on the exam paper. However well you have prepared, there is no way that you can predict exactly which poems the examiners will choose to focus on, and how the question about these poems will be worded. Your own thoughts and ideas will be recognised and valued by the examiners far more than prepared paragraphs. In other words, this guide should be seen as a

flexible tool for you to use to help shape and polish your own ideas — not a machine for turning out identical essays that don't quite do their job.

## Some useful websites

- **BBC Bitesize:** detailed notes on three representative poems by each of the four modern poets, plus five pre-1914 poems, with an interactive test on each one. www.bbc.co.uk/schools/gcsebitesize/english_literature
- **Gillian Clarke's own site**: go to For Students/Poems & Notes, then pick a poem from the alphabetical lists (A–L and M–Z). For each poem, there is a list of questions posed by students which the poet has answered. You are encouraged to submit your own questions, which may then be added to the site. www.gillianclarke.co.uk
- **The Seamus Heaney Portal**: multiple links to a brief biography, audio versions of some poems (but sadly not those featured in your *Anthology*), recordings of Heaney giving readings, and more. http://irena.blackmill.net/heaney
- **Andrew Moore's Resource Site**: brief yet comprehensive notes on all the poems in the anthology, plus all other GCSE texts. www.universalteacher.org.uk

# Context

As you read this section, ask yourself:
➢ What experiences from their own lives have Heaney and Clarke brought to their poems?
➢ How important is the background information in understanding the poems?
➢ What is interesting about the times in which the poets featured in the Pre-1914 Poetry Bank lived?

## Seamus Heaney

### Biography

Seamus Heaney was born in 1939 to a Catholic family and spent his childhood on the family farm in County Derry, Northern Ireland. He won a scholarship to St Columb's College, Derry (the school he mentions in 'Mid-Term Break') and went on to Queen's University, Belfast. He then lectured at Queen's for six years, before moving to the Republic of Ireland.

He began to publish poetry in 1966 and wrote a lot in the years that followed. His work often centres on the landscape and on his own life. In some of the poems in the *Anthology* the imagery is based on rural life, and he even uses language he remembers from his childhood. In 1971 he noted: 'I wrote about childhood because I couldn't help it' ('Out of London: Ulster's Troubles').

TopFoto

Seamus Heaney

Heaney was Professor of Poetry at the University of Oxford from 1989 to 1994 and was awarded the Nobel prize for literature in 1995. He now lives in Ireland.

## Background to the poems

Heaney alludes to the history of Ireland in a number of his poems. The following information should help you to set his ideas in context.

### Catholics and Protestants

There is a long history of tension between the Catholics and Protestants in Ireland, going back hundreds of years. On 1 July 1690 the Protestant William of Orange defeated the forces of the Catholic James II at the Battle of the Boyne. The Orange Order was formed in 1795, mainly to prevent Catholics from buying land in Protestant areas; this protected Protestant interests. Today the Orangemen march annually to commemorate the battle. They are associated with the Unionists, who wish Ireland to restore union with Great Britain.

**Key point**

Over a million people died of starvation and disease during the famine and 1.5 million emigrated to America or Canada. As a result, the population of Ireland, which had been 8 million, fell dramatically to 5.5 million. In 1847 alone, almost 250,000 people died of starvation or illnesses caused by malnutrition and 200,000 emigrated to America.

### The famine

In former centuries over half the population of Ireland depended for food on the potato crop. In autumn 1845, however, potato blight from America ruined the crop. The harvest in the wet year of 1846 was also bad, so there was nothing to eat. People were forced to eat their seed potatoes and therefore had nothing left to plant, so in 1847 there was again a poor harvest. As a result, famine ravaged the country from 1845 to 1848.

The British landowners were blamed for much of the suffering. They evicted tenants who couldn't pay rent, taxed food that was sent to Ireland from America and exported livestock and successful crops *out* of Ireland to England. The British government did nothing to help until 1847, a fact which caused widespread resentment among the Irish Catholics.

### The Troubles

At the beginning of the twentieth century the Irish nationalist organisation Sinn Fein ('We ourselves') led uprisings demanding independence from Britain. The most famous of these is the Easter Rising of 1916, when 1,500 Irish citizens attempted to seize control of Dublin and destroy British rule. After this, the British government forced through the partition of the country in a bid to retain some control. The Republic of Ireland and Northern Ireland were created in 1921 (by the Government of Ireland Act, passed in 1920). The Republic became self-governing, whereas Northern Ireland was governed mainly from Britain.

Discontent grew in Northern Ireland through the middle of the twentieth century as the Catholic majority (the Nationalists) was systematically discriminated against by the ruling Protestant minority (the Unionists). The Catholics believed they were being denied good housing and jobs. For example, in the Catholic county of Fermanagh the pay sheets of April 1969 record that the council employed 370 workers — only 32 of whom were Catholic. The Irish Republican Army (IRA), a volunteer group that had formed in the early twentieth century to fight for an independent Ireland, became active in both the north and the south.

In the late 1960s a Northern Ireland civil rights group was formed to demand fairer treatment. The reaction of the British government to the unrest was to send peace-keeping troops to Belfast and Derry. However, the peace-keeping role was undermined when curfews in Catholic areas and imprisonment without trial were

An injured man receives attention following the violence of Bloody Sunday

also brought in. The British presence went disastrously wrong on Bloody Sunday in 1972, when British troops shot dead 14 unarmed civilians. The IRA retaliated and violence escalated on both sides.

## Key point

In 1998 the Good Friday Agreement was forged between Tony Blair and Bertie Ahern, the Irish prime minister. This agreement made plans for a power-sharing government in Northern Ireland, independent of the British parliament in Westminster. It was celebrated at the time (and mentioned in Gillian Clarke's 'A Difficult Birth, Easter 1998'), although, sadly, disagreements between the IRA and the Unionists over the decommissioning of weapons later soured the process.

## Useful websites

The following websites provide further information on Ireland:

* **The Ireland Story:** www.irelandstory.com
* **World History Archives: The History of Ireland:** www.hartford-hwp.com/archives/61/index-b.html

# Gillian Clarke

## Biography

Gillian Clarke was born in Cardiff in 1937. Both her mother's and her father's families were from the countryside. She studied English at Cardiff University and worked for the BBC in London before returning to Wales in 1960. Her first poems were published in 1970, with her three main collections coming in 1982 (*Letter from a Far Country*), 1989 (*Letting in the Rumour*) and 1993 (*The King of Britain's Daughter*). Much of her work explores Welsh myths, although this aspect is not featured in the poems selected for your *Anthology*. She also writes plays, edited the *Anglo-Welsh Review* and translates Welsh writing into English. Her own poetry has been translated into ten languages. She teaches creative writing across a range of age groups, from primary school pupils to university students.

TopFoto

Gillian Clarke

She has a daughter (Catrin) and two sons and now lives with her husband on a small farm in a Welsh-speaking part of Wales, where they keep sheep. Her family and home feature in some of the *Anthology* poems.

## Background to the poems

Like Heaney, Clarke was brought up in a Christian environment, although she makes no reference to her faith in the poems featured. She does, however, refer to Christian ceremonies (such as the burial of her friend in 'October') and to a Christian festival (in 'A Difficult Birth, Easter 1998'). According to the Bible, Jesus was killed on the cross, on Good Friday, and laid in a tomb. A stone was placed in front of it. Two days later, on Easter Sunday, the stone was found rolled away from the tomb and Jesus was resurrected. In the poem, Clarke telescopes the timescale and uses the story of Jesus rising from the dead as a metaphor to show the wonder of the birth of the lambs.

### The Bosnia conflict

Bosnia was part of Yugoslavia until the country fragmented in the late 1980s. It has a multi-ethnic population of Muslim, Orthodox Christian, Roman Catholic and Jewish peoples. The ruthless president of Serbia, Slobodan Milosevic, took advantage of the chaos caused by the break-up of Yugoslavia to try to gain more land and 'purify' Serbia of Muslims and Croats. These peoples fled to Bosnia — there were 3.5 million refugees in Bosnia by October 1995.

Time Life Pictures/Getty Images

Bosnian refugees

However, some extremists in parts of Bosnia joined the Serbs in trying to kill Muslims and Croats. At first, international forces failed to intervene to stop the massacres. There was great public concern at the bloodshed and at the apparent unwillingness of the USA and Britain (among other powerful nations) to get involved. Clarke writes about the 'bleeding' fields of Bosnia in 'The Field-Mouse'.

## Useful websites

The following websites provide further information on the Bosnian conflict:

- **The Bosnian Civil War:** www.onwar.com/aced/nation/bat/bosnia/fbosnia1992.htm
- **The History Place:** www.historyplace.com/worldhistory/genocide/bosnia.htm

### Review your learning

Quick questions (answers are given on page 102

1 Which poet lives on a farm in Wales?
2 Which poet lives and works in Ireland, and features Ireland in their poetry?
3 Which poet won the Nobel prize for literature?
4 Which poet is also a translator?

Longer questions:
Do you agree with the following statements? Mark each one out of 5, where 5 means you strongly agree and 1 means you strongly disagree. Then write a short paragraph to explain your answer.

5 A poet's background is a major influence on their work.
6 It is not important for readers to know about a poet's background to understand their poems.

# Timeline

The timeline in Figure 1 shows Heaney and Clarke at the end of the range of British poets featured in your *Anthology*. As you can see, the majority of poems included in the *Anthology* were written during the nineteenth century, a particularly rich period of English literature. (However, don't assume that nothing of note was written between 1650 and 1750; the compilers of the *Anthology* simply chose not to include any of these poems.)

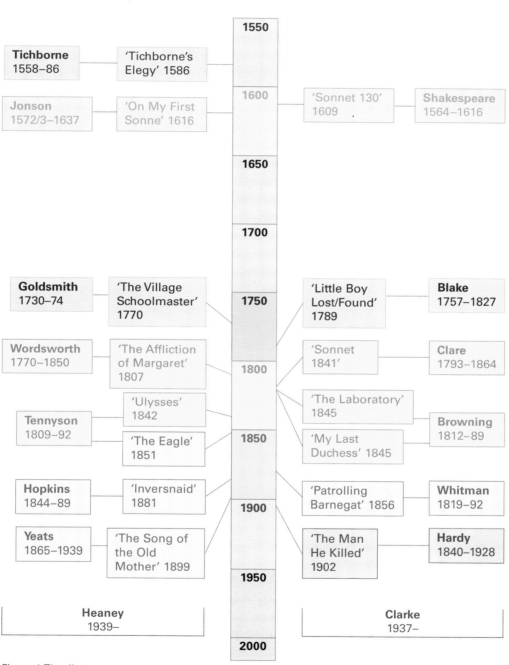

| | | |
|---|---|---|
| **Tichborne** 1558–86 | 'Tichborne's Elegy' 1586 | **1550** |
| **Jonson** 1572/3–1637 | 'On My First Sonne' 1616 | **1600** — 'Sonnet 130' 1609 — **Shakespeare** 1564–1616 |
| | | **1650** |
| | | **1700** |
| **Goldsmith** 1730–74 | 'The Village Schoolmaster' 1770 | **1750** — 'Little Boy Lost/Found' 1789 — **Blake** 1757–1827 |
| **Wordsworth** 1770–1850 | 'The Affliction of Margaret' 1807 | **1800** — 'Sonnet 1841' — **Clare** 1793–1864 |
| **Tennyson** 1809–92 | 'Ulysses' 1842 / 'The Eagle' 1851 | **1850** — 'The Laboratory' 1845 — **Browning** 1812–89 / 'My Last Duchess' 1845 |
| **Hopkins** 1844–89 | 'Inversnaid' 1881 | **1900** — 'Patrolling Barnegat' 1856 — **Whitman** 1819–92 |
| **Yeats** 1865–1939 | 'The Song of the Old Mother' 1899 | 'The Man He Killed' 1902 — **Hardy** 1840–1928 |
| **Heaney** 1939– | | **1950** — **Clarke** 1937– |
| | | **2000** |

Figure 1 Timeline

# Poem by poem
# Heaney

## 'Storm on the Island'

### What happens?

The poem describes Heaney (and other, unidentified people) sitting in a house on the edge of a cliff, during a storm. The poet shows the wild, exposed situation of the building and focuses on the emotions and fear of those inside. They are powerless against the forces of nature.

### Structure

The poem is written in **blank verse**, a form of poetry often used by Shakespeare because it sounds similar to normal speech patterns. We feel as if Heaney is speaking directly to us.

### Glossary

**stack** *(l. 4)* a haystack

**stook** *(l. 5)* a group of sheaves of corn in a field after harvest

**strafe** *(l. 17)* to bombard an enemy with shells or bombs from the air

**salvo** *(l. 17)* the simultaneous firing of artillery

### Language

The poem contains many **personal pronouns**; this emphasises its conversational style. The poet seems to be talking to us, and uses phrases like 'as you can see' (l. 4) and 'you know what I mean' (l. 7) to suggest a casual relationship with us. Yet Heaney tells us nothing about the 'We' at the opening of the poem. It is the storm outside that holds his attention rather than the people he is with. So, ironically, his use of pronouns may actually highlight his isolation.

**Enjambement** is used throughout the poem, adding to the sense of informality and casual discourse between the poet and the reader. The way the lines flow on from one to another also suggests the energy of the storm.

In fact, the **personification** of the world outside and of the elements of the storm suggests that nature itself provides the characters for the story. 'The wizened earth' (l. 3) could be seen as a poor old woman who is considerate enough not to 'trouble' the people by being sufficiently fertile to produce hay (which would be vulnerable in a storm). If there were trees, they would be 'company' (l. 6) because the noise of the wind whistling through them in the gale would make a 'tragic chorus' (l. 8). It is interesting that in a storm the barrenness of the soil is a blessing. In any other circumstance, the lack of grass and trees would be seen more as a curse.

Heaney seems prepared for the storm at the beginning of the poem and appears to have a stiff-upper-lip, confident attitude: 'We are prepared'. However, by the end he admits to feeling 'fear'. He must have seen storms many times — the fact that the people build their houses 'squat' (l. 1) shows that storms are expected, and because the title is 'Storm on the Island', not '*A Storm*', we assume that storms are relatively common. Despite all the preparation and all his experience, the poet cannot help being frightened. The power of nature is still dominant.

## Imagery

The poet uses a **simile** to describe the sea spray: '[spitting] like a tame cat/Turned savage' (ll. 15–16). Why do you think Heaney uses an image of a pet becoming wild to portray the wildness of the storm?

He also uses **metaphor** to emphasise the power and violence of the storm — the military imagery at the end of the poem ('strafes', 'salvo', 'bombarded': ll. 17–18). This suggests that Heaney sees nature as being violent; perhaps he is also making a link between nature and the Irish political situation.

**Pause for thought**

Do you feel that Heaney is awe-struck by the storm? He admits to feeling fear, but does he feel some admiration for it too?

## Ideas to consider

* The poem shows vividly the power of nature — and man's powerlessness to control it. It is all we can do to survive.
* Perhaps Heaney also wants us to consider the political storm on the island of Ireland, with all the violence the Troubles have brought to the Irish people. He feels as powerless to do anything about the Irish situation as he does about fighting against nature.

# 'Perch'

## What happens?

Heaney describes fish in the Bann River, near his home. He sees them now, as a grown-up, in the same way that he saw them as a child; they, and the river, appear unchanged. He uses a variety of often humorous, contrasting images to depict the perch.

### Glossary

**Bann River** *(l. 1)* a river in Northern Ireland, famous for coarse fishing
**slub** *(l. 3)* a lump in wool, yarn or thread
**runty** *(l. 3)* undersized; of thick-set build

## Structure

This ten-line poem is actually just one complete sentence, divided into five **rhyming couplets**. The couplets flow from one to another, suggesting the continuous, uninterrupted movement of the water. The rhymes are not obvious ('slur'/'air', 'ready'/'body' — this is called **half-rhyme**), so that the poem is not dominated by the rhyme scheme. The rhymes create an echo effect and give energy. There is repetition within the lines, such as 'finland... fenland' (l. 8), and sounds resonate across the couplets, as in 'adoze...Guzzling' (ll. 6–7).

## Language

There is a mixture of **alliteration** and **assonance**, sometimes suggesting the uneven rush of the water and sometimes suggesting something about the character of the perch. For instance in line 3 the 'u' sounds in '"grunts", little flood-slubs, runty' hint at the solid weight of the perch, while the repeated 'r' in 'runty and ready' sounds like running water. Heaney also suggests the flow of the water by using **enjambement**, as in 'on air/That is water' (ll. 8–9).

### Pause for thought

Using highlighter pens, mark all the examples of alliteration you can find in one colour and all the examples of assonance in another.

Heaney enjoys using **word-play** and **puns** in the poem, as in 'Perch on their water-perch' (l. 1), which likens the fish to birds; and 'In the finland of perch' (l. 8), which suggests (since all fish have fins) that the river is their country, like Finland. This light-hearted approach shows his affection for the perch and how amused he is by them.

As well as the perch, the river itself is described. It is 'clear', with a 'clay bank' and alders overhanging the water (ll. 1–2). (Perhaps the shadows of the overhanging branches create the 'perches' for the fish to rest on.) It appears a tranquil, idealised place — a 'glorified body' (l. 4). Heaney wants to remind himself that some places remain still and perfect in today's rushed world.

The poem is written in the **present tense** — even though it is as much about what Heaney remembers from his childhood as what he sees as an adult. This makes the poem immediate, and shows that what was important to Heaney years ago is still important now.

## Imagery

The perch are not once described as being fish. They are described instead through a range of **metaphors**. For example, in 'they're bluntly holding the pass' (l. 5), they are seen as troops stoutly defending a mountain pass in the face of an opposing army. This emphasises how strong the perch seem and how determined they are to stay in position. It is interesting, though, that in the next line the perch are 'adoze', an idea suggesting laziness, which contrasts with the previous military image.

The river is described in metaphors too. It is the river that is seen as the opposing army in the quotation above, which is ironic, as the water is the perch's home — not something that they need to combat. The homeliness of the river is emphasised by its providing a 'water-roof' (l. 6) and 'carpets' (l. 9).

### Pause for thought

Try to find at least four *different* metaphors portraying the perch.

Look for some of the other metaphors used to describe the river.

## Ideas to consider

- There is a sense of permanence and optimism in the poem — the perch are still there, 'on hold' (l. 9), exactly as the poet remembers them from his childhood, despite all the flux and change in the world. Heaney feels comforted by this.
- He seems very affectionate towards the perch — even though some of his images are not very flattering. There is humour in the contrasting metaphors.
- Although the perch seem still and unmoving, they are really moving all the time against the flow of the river. They are constantly fighting the current, 'all muscle and slur' (l. 7), to stay in the shade of the alders. Maybe Heaney is hinting that not all in life is as it first appears.

'Alder-dapple and waver'

# 'Blackberry-Picking'

## What happens?

Heaney remembers late summers when he was a boy, going blackberrying with other children. The fruit was so delicious and the children were so greedy that each year they filled a whole bathtub with berries. However, the berries soon became mildewed and spoilt. The young Heaney was always disappointed when this happened, even though he knew it was inevitable.

## Structure

The poem is composed of **rhyming couplets**. The rhymes are not always obvious ('sweet'/'in it', 'drills'/'full' — this is called **half-rhyme**), so that the poem is not dominated by the rhyme scheme. The final couplet provides the only true rhyme and is particularly conclusive as a result. Heaney chose this pattern because it is typical of children's poetry and because, traditionally, rhyming couplets were used for tragic tales.

### Glossary

**Philip Hobsbaum** a poet and critic who set up creative writing groups, one of which Heaney joined. (He is *not* the 'You' in l. 5)

**Bluebeard** (*l.16*) a character from a traditional fairy tale who marries many times; mysteriously, each wife disappears. It is finally discovered that he is murdering them

**byre** (*l.17*) a cow shed

**cache** (*l.19*) a secret store, hiding place

## Language

The rural setting for the poem is clearly drawn. Heaney describes the farm's 'hayfields, cornfields and potato-drills' (l. 11); the children store the berries in the 'byre' (l. 17).

The poem is written in the first person and is apparently autobiographical. We are not told who 'You' (l. 5) is: Heaney could as easily be talking directly to the reader as to one of his friends. We are not told anything about the children, apart from their love of blackberries and how their greed turns to disillusionment. We might feel close to the poet because he is talking to us so directly, or distant from him because we know so little about him and his companions.

The poem appeals to the senses: we can almost *see* the delicious blackberries ('glossy purple clot': l. 3), *smell* and *taste* them ('sweet/Like thickened wine': ll. 5–6), *hear* them 'tinkling' into the children's buckets (l. 13) — and *feel* the briars scratch (l. 10). This makes us very involved in the poem; we can imagine being there too.

The language describing the ripe berries is very sensual and the children's desire for them is expressed in adult language. The berries are described as tasting 'Like thickened wine', a drink it is unlikely the children would have experienced at that age. They have a 'lust' (l. 7) for the fruit — a word which is usually associated with sexual desire, something the children would also not have known.

However, the berries cause pain as well as arousing joy (the 'briars scratched': l. 10) and collecting them is destructive ('wet grass bleached our boots': l. 10). Later in the poem the berries themselves are destroyed by the 'rat-grey fungus' (l. 19).

Heaney shows us the natural cycle of a blackberry, turning from 'green' to 'red' (l. 4), then 'ink[ing] up' (l. 8) (turning black) until they are perfect. Once they are picked, however, they begin the natural process of decay, becoming 'stinking' (l. 20) and 'sour' (l. 21). Heaney reminds us at the beginning (ll. 1–2) that the berries only ripen in the right conditions. Maybe, because they have such a short life, they are even more desirable.

## Imagery

The poet creates a near onomatopoeic effect at times, and the poem contains many phrases where **sound** has an effect. The 'k' sounds in 'We trekked and picked' (l. 12) are heavy and suggest the amount of effort the children had to put in.

Heaney uses several striking **similes**. For instance, the full pails appeared 'Like a plate of eyes' (l. 15), a startling, sinister description of something they all craved so much. Perhaps this hints at the destruction to come.

**Metaphors** are also used effectively, such as 'Our hands were peppered/With thorn pricks' (ll. 15–16). This reminds us of the spicy heat of pepper — and hence the pain the children experienced — and the way the tiny grains of pepper are almost invisible, as the thorn pricks would have been.

### Pause for thought

The poem contains images of blood, in 'summer's blood was in it' (l. 6) and the reference to Bluebeard, whose palms were sticky with the blood of his wives. Why do you think Heaney chose this fairytale image?

## Ideas to consider

- The huge waste of rotten fruit is caused by the children's greed. They picked far more berries than they could eat. Perhaps Heaney is making the simple point that those who are most greedy have the most to lose. Maybe he feels guilty.
- The children are seen as innocent and enthusiastic, but at the same time they are learning important lessons for adulthood, such as acceptance when something goes wrong.
- It is interesting that the children apparently pick the blackberries 'Each year' (l. 24), and each year see their hoard turn rotten. They have not learnt from the previous disappointment. It is a cycle: their excitement in finding the fruit and their sadness at its loss are constantly repeated.
- Perhaps Heaney is hinting that often life contains disappointments like this one.

### Pause for thought

Is Heaney suggesting that *all* pleasure turns to disappointment after a while?

# 'Death of a Naturalist'

## What happens?

The poet remembers as a child investigating the nature he saw around the flax-dam. He liked watching the insects, but 'best of all' (l. 8) he liked the frogspawn, and would collect it every year so he could watch it turn into tadpoles. He learnt about a frog's life cycle at school too. However, one day he saw a swarm of frogs invade the dam. He was terrified by them and was suddenly frightened that they had come to gain revenge for all his years of collecting their spawn.

### Glossary

**flax** *(l. 1)* the plant from which linen is made

**flax-dam** *(l. 1)* a pool where bundles of flax are laid for a few weeks to soften their stems, in the first stage of the linen-making process. The bundles are weighted down by large sods (lumps of soil and turf)

**townland** *(l. 2)* a small administrative area in Northern Ireland, a section of a parish. Townlands are often bordered by streams, old hedges and old roads

## Structure

The poem is written in **blank verse** so that it sounds like everyday speech. It is divided into two stanzas: the first deals with the poet's happy, innocent exploration of nature, the second focuses on the shocking event that changed his views.

## Language

There is **enjambement** throughout the poem, so that the lines run into one another and sound like everyday speech.

The language is full of **vocabulary** to do with **decay**, including 'festered', 'rotted', 'sweltered' (ll. 1–4), 'rank' (l. 22). This sets the scene for Heaney's nightmare.

 **Pause for thought**

Did Heaney deserve what happened? Think about the poem's title. What exactly do you think has died?

There are **childish words**, 'slobber' (l. 8) and 'jellied/Specks' (ll. 11–12), for example, to help us see things through the young Heaney's eyes — and some daring, unexpected words, like 'farting' (l. 30), which shows us how affected he was. There are also words that adults use when speaking *to* children; his teacher, Miss Walls, said 'mammy frog', 'little eggs' (ll. 17–18).

Heaney uses **alliteration** to emphasise the intensity of the experiences he describes, such as 'heavy headed' (l. 2), 'jampotfuls of the jellied/Specks' (ll. 11–12), 'coarse croaking' (l. 25). There is also some **repetition** — 'dragonflies...butterflies' (l. 7), 'bullfrog...mammy frog...Frogspawn' (ll. 16–19) — which creates echoes in the poem and further heightens the richness of the experiences.

There is **onomatopoeia**, as in 'gargled' (l. 5), 'croaking' (l. 25) and 'plop' (l. 29), so we can imagine the sounds surrounding the child. In the second stanza particularly, the noises are alarming, like 'obscene threats' (l. 29).

We are lulled into a false sense of security by the descriptions of the activities Heaney enjoyed as a child — he collected frogspawn 'every spring' (l. 10) and there is a sense of permanence about the fact that the 'flax-dam' was there 'All year' (l. 1). This security is destroyed in stanza 2, on 'one hot day' (l. 22) when he was frightened by the frogs. It is a dramatic **contrast**.

## Imagery

The poem includes some striking imagery. Early on, Heaney uses a **simile** in the affectionate description, 'frogspawn that grew like clotted water' (l. 9). It reminds us of clotted cream. Compare this to the simile describing the frogs 'Poised like mud grenades' (l. 30) in stanza 2. Here, Heaney's words suggest danger and fear.

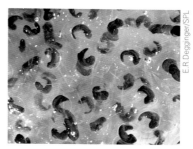

What Heaney had enjoyed 'best of all', the frogspawn, became his downfall

There are also effective **metaphors**. In stanza 2, the frogs 'were cocked/On sods' (ll. 27–28), an image which likens frogs to guns, cocked and ready to shoot. Nowadays, this might suggest the frogs were suicide bombers, ready to use their own bodies as weapons.

The imagery taken all together suggests that the frogs were on the warpath. In the second stanza they were 'angry', they 'Invaded the flax-dam' (ll. 23–24), they were 'gross-bellied' (l. 27), they seemed to make 'obscene threats'. Heaney describes the frogs in such violent terms to illustrate the intensity of his fear.

The sun itself seems a malevolent force — the flax 'sweltered' in its 'punishing' heat (l. 4), intensifying the putrid smells; and the incident with the swarm of frogs occurred on 'one hot day' (l. 22). In a strange way, perhaps the sun is in league with the frogs.

## Pause for thought

Do you think there is a link between the violence of the frogs in stanza 2, which destroyed the young Heaney's innocence, and the violence in Northern Ireland that destroyed the peace there?

## Ideas to consider

* Compare how Heaney felt about frogs at first — he was almost affectionate towards them and proud of how much he knew about them — to how he saw them on that 'one hot day', when they suddenly become the enemy and he the victim.
* There is an abrupt shift. What Heaney had enjoyed 'best of all', the frogspawn, became his nemesis, or downfall. He suddenly felt that he was going to have to pay the price of all the pleasure he'd had, as the frogs sought their revenge.

# 'Digging'

## What happens?

As Heaney sits inside, writing, he sees his elderly father outside digging the flowerbeds. This reminds Heaney of his childhood, when his father worked in the potato fields, and of even earlier, when *his* father cut turf. Heaney's father and grandfather were both experts and worked hard. Heaney considers whether he is following the family tradition, not by digging with a spade, but by 'digging' with his pen.

### Glossary

**drills** *(l. 8)* ridges with small furrows on top for sowing seeds; here, the rows of potato plants

**lug** *(l. 10)* the part of the spade to which the handle is fixed

**turf** *(l.17)* peat for fuel, cut in slabs or blocks

## Structure

The poem is divided into nine irregular stanzas of between two and five lines. Perhaps the irregularity suggests the random nature of Heaney's thoughts. It begins with two pairs of rhyming couplets, but this pattern is not repeated — the rhymes disappear, so that the poem sounds more like natural speech.

## Language

The poem moves from the **present tense** (ll. 1–8) to the **past tense** (ll. 9–24), then back to the present (ll. 25–30) as Heaney reflects on his memories. However, it concludes in the **future tense**, 'I'll dig', to show that he is determined to carry on working and writing.

It is the 'clean rasping sound' (l. 3) of his father's digging that first alerts Heaney. Sound is important in the poem and he uses **onomatopoeia** (and near-onomatopoeia) to suggest the 'gravelly ground' (l. 4) and the 'squelch and slap' (l. 25) of the peat, to make the images more vivid.

**Enjambement** is used to make the poem more dramatic. Between lines 5 and 6 enjambement shows the plunge through the years from the present to 'twenty years away' in line 7. Between lines 21 and 22 it shows the keenness of his grandfather to get back to work after a short break.

The spade has become almost a part of Heaney's father, with his boot 'nestled on the

Heaney remembers his own part in the potato harvest

lug' and his knee 'levered firmly' against the shaft (ll. 10–11). The use of these **technical terms** shows that he is an expert at his job. 'Shaft' and 'levered' even suggest he is like a machine. Similarly, the exact description of the poet's grandfather at work, 'Nicking and slicing neatly, heaving sods' (l. 22) shows his expertise. You hear the rhythm of the spade in the repeated '–ing' sounds.

Including the title, 'dig' or 'digging' is used five times through the poem; 'spade' is used three times. The words are like a refrain, emphasising their importance to each generation. The three men earn their livelihoods from their own particular type of digging.

## Imagery

There is a **simile** in the opening couplet: 'The squat pen rests; snug as a gun' (l. 2). This suggests that the pen is strong and powerful and fits Heaney's hand exactly. Although the poem was written in 1966, before the Troubles, the gun image might also hint that Heaney had been about to write something destructive. In that case, he changed tack when he saw his father being constructive, creating beauty in the flower bed outside.

**Pause for thought**

Does Heaney feel embarrassed that he is not labouring in the same way that his father and grandfather did?

The remembered scene is so vivid to Heaney that the scents ('cold smell of potato mould'), sights ('curt cuts of an edge') and sounds ('squelch and slap') of the men digging (ll. 25–26) 'awaken in my head'. Heaney uses sensual imagery to make the scene real to us. Yet there is an overtone of violence here: he points out that the spade cuts 'Through living roots' (l. 27).

## Ideas to consider

- Heaney is clearly affectionate towards both men. There is sympathy as he describes his father's 'straining rump' (l. 6) and remembers his own part in the potato harvest, 'Loving their cool hardness in our hands' (l. 14). There is admiration in the colloquial exclamation: 'By God, the old man could handle a spade' (l. 15). He is proud of them both, too. We can imagine the young Heaney boasting to his school friends that his 'grandfather cut more turf in a day/Than any other man' (ll. 17–18). Perhaps Heaney feels regretful that he is not following in his father's and grandfather's footsteps. On the other hand, maybe he is proud of what he does instead.

**Pause for thought**

How do you think his father feels (and his grandfather would have felt) about Heaney's literary career? What do you feel Heaney 'digs up' through his writing?

# 'Mid-Term Break'

## What happens?

This poem is about the sudden death of Heaney's younger brother, Christopher, who was killed in a road accident when he was only four years old. The teenage Heaney has to be brought home from boarding school. He is embarrassed to see his father crying and to be singled out by local mourners. It is only the following day, when Heaney has the chance to be alone with his brother's body, that he feels calm enough to grieve.

## Structure

The poem consists of seven three-line stanzas, followed by a final single beautiful line. There is no rhyme scheme (apart from the closing couplet), so the poem resembles natural speech.

## Language

There seems to be a divide in the poem between the fifth and sixth stanzas (ll. 15–16). The first section of the poem is full of events that were triggered by Christopher's death, such as the gathering of family and friends and his mother's 'angry tearless sighs' (l. 13). It is full of **active verbs**. The second section concentrates on the dead body. It is much calmer and quieter.

The word 'knelling' (l. 2) immediately suggests that a death is involved, because, although it refers to the school bell, knelling is usually associated with funerals. We are encouraged to read on, to find out what has happened.

We realise that it is a close relative of Heaney who has died — not until the end do we know it is his younger brother and discover *how* he died.

Only one character in the tragedy is given a name, Big Jim Evans, presumably a family friend. Everyone else is **anonymous** ('our neighbours', 'The baby', 'old men', 'strangers', 'the nurses') and Heaney also refers to his parents formally as 'my father' and 'my mother'. We are never even told the name of the dead child — perhaps personalising the poem with names would make it all too raw.

There is a lot of **awkwardness** when Heaney reaches home. He feels uncomfortable to meet his 'father crying' (l. 4); 'The baby cooed and laughed' (l. 7), which

### Pause for thought

Look again at the title of the poem. A 'break' is usually a holiday — a happy time. Why do you think Heaney used this misleading phrase?

seems inappropriate to the occasion. Heaney is aware that people are explaining to 'strangers' who he is. (They are only strangers to Heaney, who knows fewer local people now he is at boarding school.)

The awkward atmosphere is emphasised by the use of **euphemisms**. The old men say they are 'sorry for my trouble' (l. 10). 'Big Jim Evans' kindly saying 'it was a hard blow' (l. 6) is particularly bitter as it was indeed the 'hard blow' from a car that killed the child. The formal word 'corpse' (l. 15) acts almost as a euphemism, avoiding the fact that a loved one has died.

From line 16, however, the awkwardness and euphemisms end; the language becomes **calm** and **lyrical**. Heaney describes the room where his brother's body is lying, and the body itself in detail. He does not describe his own feelings, but we can gain a sense of his emotions through the description and imagery.

## Imagery

Although Heaney **personifies** the 'Snowdrops/And candles' which 'soothed the bedside' (ll. 16–17), we know that they actually helped to soothe *him*.

All the items in the bedroom that Heaney chooses to describe are significant. They **symbolise** important ideas:

- Snowdrops are white and so suggest the innocence and purity of the child. Visually, they also suggest the waxy whiteness of the dead child's skin.
- Candles light the bedside. Candles are associated with churches and death, but also with romance. Perhaps they show the love Heaney had for his brother.
- The bruise is likened to a 'poppy' (l. 19). Since the First World War poppies have been symbols of death, but it is also interesting that the drug opium is derived from poppies. Perhaps the child is now free of pain, through death.

Heaney avoids using the word 'coffin', using instead the **simile** 'He lay in the four foot box as in his cot' (l. 20). This suggests the child is perfectly at rest.

The closing couplet is very powerful. The repetition in the last line emphasises the smallness and vulnerability of the child, while the rhyme heightens the finality of what has happened.

## Ideas to consider

- It is interesting that Heaney makes the poem seem so personal without actually describing his emotions. The detailed descriptions of the mourners and the symbolism when describing his brother's bedroom show his grief, so he avoids the sentimentality often found in poems about death.
- The death was a key event for the poet. As well as having to cope with losing a brother, Heaney suddenly had to grow up and become more responsible. He saw his strong father 'crying' and helpless, and knew his mother 'held [his] hand' for support (l. 12).

# 'Follower'

## What happens?

Heaney remembers how, as a child, he loved to follow his father as he ploughed the fields with his team of horses. His father was an expert and the young Heaney was inspired to follow in his footsteps and become a farmer too. By the end of the poem, however, the roles have been partly reversed. Heaney did *not* go to work on the land — and now his father is 'stumbling/Behind' *him* (ll. 23–24) .

## Structure

The poem is made up of six regular four-lined stanzas (**quatrains**). The regularity of the verse reminds us of the precise, regular furrows Heaney's father ploughed. This regularity is heightened by the alternate rhyme scheme (ABAB). As Heaney has used **enjambement** and **half-rhyme** ('plough'/'furrow'), however, the rhyme scheme is subtle and does not jar with the gentle, fluid feel of the poem.

## Language

Heaney provides us with **technical terms** used in ploughing (see the 'Glossary' above) which impress us. It proves that the task is a skilled one, specialised enough to have its own **lexicon** (or bank of words).

His father is 'An expert' (l. 5). Heaney puts this short phrase at the beginning of a stanza to add emphasis: it suggests there is nothing more to be said.

It is interesting that Heaney's father appears to work effortlessly, turning his team 'with a single pluck/Of reins', while the horses are 'sweating' (ll. 8–9).

There is a **contrast** between his father's control and concentration ('His eye/Narrowed and angled at the ground': ll. 10–11) and Heaney's own lack of control ('I stumbled': l. 13; 'tripping, falling,/Yapping': ll. 21–22).

Most of the poem is in the **past tense**, but we are suddenly brought into the **present** in line 22: 'But today'. Heaney cannot ignore his father's presence.

## Imagery

Heaney has used **nautical imagery** throughout the poem. Each image heightens our appreciation of his father's strength and skill.

* 'His shoulders globed like a full sail' (l. 2): this **simile** suggests the rounded shape of Heaney's father as he controls the plough, and emphasises his strength. He is powering the plough through the soil as a sail powers a ship.

- 'The sod rolled over without breaking' (l. 7): a wave would break, but the ploughman's skill is such that the sod *doesn't* break. The wave image also reminds us of how shiny and glossy the soil is when it is freshly turned, catching the light almost like water.
- 'Mapping the furrow exactly' (l. 12): this suggests that Heaney's father is setting his course as carefully as if he were a ship's navigator.
- 'I stumbled in his … wake' (l. 13): the young Heaney follows his father's 'ship', just as small craft and seagulls sometimes follow a boat out to sea.
- 'Dipping and rising' (l. 16): Heaney likens himself to a small boat bobbing around in the waves created by larger, more important vessels.

## Ideas to consider

- There seems to have been great affection between father and son. Heaney's father would let him '[ride] on his back' (l. 15), and tolerated him even though he was a 'nuisance' (l. 21). Heaney clearly idolised his father: 'All I ever did was follow' (l. 19). Do you think that the affection between father and son remains now that Heaney has grown up?

## Pause for thought

Heaney's father 'will not go away' (l. 24). Does Heaney feel frustrated and embarrassed by his father's helpless-ness, or is he accepting of it?

- The word 'follow' is used both literally and metaphorically. Not only did the child Heaney follow his father about his work, he also wanted to follow him into farming: 'I wanted to grow up and plough' (l. 17). Heaney was inspired by his father, yet did not, in the end, become a farmer. Do you think he feels guilty?
- It is not made clear whether his father is really there with Heaney (with Heaney looking after him), or whether it is the *thought* of his father that Heaney cannot escape from.

# 'At a Potato Digging'

## What happens?

The poem is divided into four sections:

I Heaney describes a modern-day potato harvest: a mechanical digger turns up the potatoes, but the crop is collected by hand. People are bent over the soil, filling their baskets with potatoes. Even today, people are conscious of the famine that occurred over 150 years ago.

II Heaney then describes the potatoes themselves. The different varieties are different colours. The harvest is good and 'solid': *these* potatoes do not contain blight.

III This section remembers the horrors of the famine, describing how apparently good potatoes rotted within three days. As a consequence of the loss of millions of potatoes, millions of people starved.

IV We are brought back to the present day, where the potato pickers *do* have food. Yet we wonder whether they are superstitious. They seem to make offerings to the gods, to guard against another famine.

### Glossary

**drill** *(ll. 1 and 22)* a ridge with a furrow on top for sowing seeds; here, the row of potato plants
**creels** *(l. 4)* large baskets
**headland** *(l. 6)* the strip left unploughed at the end of a field
**pit** *(l. 8)* where the potatoes are stored
**humus** *(l. 25)* rotted plant matter in the soil
**'forty-five** *(l. 32)* 1845, the start of the Irish famine
**libations** *(l. 57)* drinks offered to the gods

## Structure

The sections are structured differently:

Sections I and IV (the sections that deal with today's harvest) both consist of four-line stanzas (quatrains) that rhyme ABAB. The regular pattern echoes the routine of the work and the regularity of the annual task (it 'Recurs mindlessly as autumn' l. 13). Interestingly, the final stanza breaks the rhyme scheme with 'fasts'/'crumbs' at the conclusion of the poem.

Section II consists of one seven-line stanza followed by one six-line stanza. There is some rhyme but the pattern is not regular, perhaps to show the irregularity of nature and the fact that no two potatoes are the same.

Section III is also made up of quatrains, but the lines are only seven syllables long, shorter than the pentameters (ten-syllable lines) of sections I and IV. Their brevity reminds us of the scarcity of food; even the poetry seems starved. They rhyme AABB.

## Language

The poem is about harvest time, usually a time of celebration. Yet the language in this poem is hardly celebratory. In the first stanza the digger is violent — it 'wrecks the drill' and the pickers' fingers are 'dead in the cold'. Heaney sets a

**sinister tone**, which is developed in section III when he describes the effect of the potato blight. The picture painted in this third section is very vivid: 'Stinking potatoes fouled the land,/pits turned pus into filthy mounds' (ll. 46–7) — it is a nightmare vision.

**Religion** is important. Yet it is not Catholicism that Heaney writes about, but a pagan faith. The pickers, bent over the soil, seem to be praying, but not to the Christian God. They are paying 'homage to the famine god' (l. 14). Their work is seen as a religious ritual, a petition for food, that has taken place over 'Centuries'. At the end of the poem, as the pickers eat their lunch, the spilt tea and crumbs of bread are seen as offerings to the god.

**Alliteration** is used effectively to link ideas, such as 'A higgledy line from hedge to headland' (l. 6). The repeated 'h' sound makes us think of people breathing heavily as they work.

There is also **repetition**. For example, section IV ironically uses 'deadens' and 'Dead-beat', when describing the pickers.

### Pause for thought

Do you feel that the pickers' homage to the famine god is more important for them than an organised religion (such as Catholicism)?

TopFoto

The interior of a peasant's cottage during the potato famine

## Imagery

There are **metaphors** and **similes** throughout the poem. The imagery is all based on **nature**, to echo the setting and subject of the poem. Here are some examples taken from each section of the poem.

### Section I

* 'Labourers swarm behind' (l. 3). This metaphor likens pickers to insects, perhaps ants, scurrying along. It suggests that there are a great many of them.
* 'Like crows attacking crow-black fields' (l. 5). The simile seems ironic, because it likens the pickers to scavenger birds on the attack, when really they are simply collecting food. Perhaps 'attacking' shows the pickers' desperation to gather all the supplies in. As in the previous image, the pickers are made to seem small and insignificant, and lack individuality. The soil is 'black' and rich.
* 'hands fumble towards the black/Mother' (ll. 11–12). The 'black Mother' is a metaphor for the soil. The soil produces living things — it is, in a way, the mother of the potatoes, an idea which is continued in line 26, 'a clean birth'. Heaney is suggesting that the soil is in some ways our mother too, as the soil, like a parent, provides us with food.

### Section II

* 'scattered/like inflated pebbles' (ll. 17–18). This simile reminds us of the shape of the potatoes, hard and knobbly like pebbles.
* 'Split/by the spade, they show white as cream' (ll. 22–23). This simile describes potatoes sliced in half by a spade — the inside is creamy white. We associate cream with luxury, and so Heaney asks us not to take this common-place vegetable for granted. There have been periods in history when it was indeed a luxury item.
* 'a clean birth' (l. 26). The potatoes in this metaphor are born from the earth. Like a baby, they come from the darkness into the light. In a way, we love the food that sustains us as we would love a new-born child.
* 'Live skulls, blind-eyed' (l. 29). This metaphor suggests that the potatoes are large (as big as skulls) and fertile ('blind-eyed' shows that the eyes, or sprouts, have not yet grown). They are like new-born children, almost blinking in the light.

### Section III

* 'Live skulls, blind-eyed' (l. 30). The link between sections II and III is striking. The phrase that is used at the end of section II is repeated immediately afterwards to begin section III, but here the words are taken literally: the starving Irish are so emaciated that their heads are no more than 'Live skulls…balanced on/wild higgledy skeletons'.

- 'beaks of famine snipped at guts' (l. 41). Hunger pangs are likened to pecking birds in this chilling metaphor, cutting into the stomachs of the starving people. It links to the image of emaciated faces resembling 'plucked bird[s]' two lines before.
- 'Hope rotted like a marrow' (l. 45). In this simile, Heaney reminds us that all food decays. A marrow is a large vegetable with a high water content that rots away to nothing; the Irish had a lot of hope to begin with, but all hope died as they starved.

### Section IV

- 'a gay flotilla of gulls' (l. 50). In contrast to the drabness and blackness of the previous sections, Heaney presents us with cheerful gulls that seem to sail overhead.
- 'The rhythm deadens' (l. 51). As lunchtime approaches, the rhythm of the workers gets slower. The use of the word 'deadens' is significant, given the suffering and death described in section III.
- 'breaking timeless fasts' (l. 55). The pickers' break for lunch symbolises the first food that the people had eaten since the famine. They eat 'Down in the ditch', where people used to die of hunger.

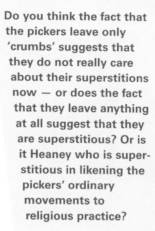

**Pause for thought**

Do you think the fact that the pickers leave only 'crumbs' suggests that they do not really care about their superstitions now — or does the fact that they leave anything at all suggest that they are superstitious? Or is it Heaney who is superstitious in likening the pickers' ordinary movements to religious practice?

## Ideas to consider

- The potato famine of 150 years ago still seems very real to today's pickers. Why do you feel it is important for them not to forget it?
- What does Heaney feel about the famine?

# Poem by poem
# Clarke

## 'Catrin'

### What happens?

The poem is about Clarke's daughter, Catrin. Clarke remembers awaiting her birth in the hospital and the birth itself: it was a 'struggle to become/Separate'. Now that Catrin is much older, there is still a sense of struggle between mother and daughter. Catrin is asking her mother for permission to skate in the dark, and Clarke feels bound to her daughter by an invisible umbilical cord, not knowing whether to let her free.

### Structure

The poem is split into two unequal stanzas. They are divided by subject matter rather than by a set poetic form. One deals with Catrin's birth, one with her as a young teenager. The pause between stanzas 1 and 2 adds tension: we wonder what happens as a result of the birth. The lines are fairly short, which enables Clarke to make clear statements ('I can remember you, child'), so adding drama to the poem. We might even see the long, narrow form of the poem as a visual image of an umbilical cord.

### Language

The poem is written in the **first person**, which makes it immediate.

It begins in the **present tense**, moves to the **past tense** as Clarke recalls her daughter's birth, then returns to the present in line 20 ('Still I am fighting'), as she agonises over whether to allow Catrin to go out again or not. Again, this makes the poem immediate: we feel involved in the dilemma.

Much of the poem's language deals with **conflict**, such as 'our first/Fierce confrontation' (ll. 6–7), 'struggle' (ll.15 and 18) and 'defiant' (l. 24). Yet there is also language of **love**: 'Red rope of love' (l. 8) and 'tender' (l. 14). The 'struggle' of birth becomes symbolic of the later struggles in a parent–child relationship. Clarke seems to be saying that a parent experiences both extremes of feeling. It is possible that the greater the love is, the greater the conflict, as it is the parent's instinct to protect the child that causes the conflict between them.

Clarke describes the ordinary, everyday things that went on outside the hospital, such as 'cars taking/Turn at the traffic lights' (ll. 4–5), in **contrast** to the momentous thing that was happening to her inside the hospital.

Lines 11–16 are confusing. Clarke states that she 'wrote/All over the walls', but we know this is not a literal description. Perhaps she felt that what she said or shouted during labour was so intense that the words wrote themselves into the walls. Remember that she is a poet, so she often portrays ideas through writing.

**Enjambement** is used effectively several times in the poem, such as between lines 15 and 16, 'to become/Separate'. The word 'separate' is on a new line, physically separated from the rest of the sentence. It enacts the idea it describes.

Clarke uses **alliteration** at times to link her ideas, as in: 'coloured the clean squares' and 'circles/Of our struggle' (ll. 13–15).

The description of Catrin the teenager is signif-icant. Her hair is 'straight, strong, long' and she has a 'rosy/Defiant glare' (ll. 22–24). The accumulation of **adjectives** suggests someone who is confident and forceful.

## Pause for thought

Which do you feel is stronger in the poem, love or conflict?

## Imagery

The umbilical cord is described twice in the poem. It is 'the tight/Red rope of love (ll. 7–8) in the first stanza, but merely 'that old rope' (l. 25) in the second. Red reminds us both of romance (red roses and Valentine hearts) and of blood. The **metaphor** might make us think of a rope in a tug-of-war competition, linking to the conflict theme. We may also think of the ropes of DNA that connect a parent with a child. Clarke seems to suggest that an invisible umbilical cord ties parents to their children even as the children grow up.

Clarke also uses metaphor to describe the hospital. It is 'a square/ Environmental blank' (ll. 9–10), sterile and plain. Later on it is 'the glass tank' (l. 19). Clarke's imagery illustrates the blandness and starkness of the building, at odds with the overwhelming emotion that it contains.

## Ideas to consider

- On her website, www.gillianclarke.co.uk, the poet says that the subject of 'Catrin' is 'Why did my beautiful baby have to become a teenager?' Do you feel that this resentful, wistful idea comes across in the poem?
- What is the tone of the first line? Practise saying the line aloud. Should 'child' be spoken affectionately, to emphasise the maternal love Clarke feels for Catrin? Or should it be said with bitterness, indicating all the pain that motherhood involves?
- The daughter sees the excitement of skating in the dark; her mother sees the danger. Whose viewpoint do we experience most clearly at the end of the poem — the mother's or the daughter's?

# 'Baby-sitting'

## What happens?

Clarke describes a night when she is baby-sitting for a child she does not know well. She describes her own lack of feeling towards the child (in comparison with her feelings towards her own child). She imagines the baby's terror if she were to wake up: the child would feel abandoned and alone. Clarke feels sorry for the child, knowing there is nothing she could do to help her.

## Structure

The poem consists of two ten-line stanzas, the first dealing with Clarke's attitude towards the child, the second with the child's attitude towards her.

## Language

The poem is written in the **first person**, which makes it immediate.

The poem starts in the **present tense**, as Clarke describes her situation. It moves into the **future tense** in line 7 when she imagines what will happen when the child wakes up. (She *could* have used the conditional tense: 'To her I *might* represent absolute abandonment'; she opts for the more definite future to show she has no doubt at all about the baby's reaction.)

Ingram

Clarke's description of the baby implies that she is beautiful, but to the poet she is only 'perfectly acceptable'

The language is full of **absolutes**: 'I am afraid of her' (l. 6), 'She will hate me' (l. 7), 'It will not come' (l. 20). This reinforces Clarke's absolute certainty of what will happen if the baby wakes up: she will be powerless to do anything that might help the child.

We are **shocked** by Clarke's initial description of the baby as 'wrong' and the stark statement, 'I don't love/This baby' (ll. 1–2). Yet the idea that Clarke doesn't love *this* baby implies that there is another baby (a 'right' one) that she *does* love: that she is a mother herself. She is showing that although the baby is 'Roseate' and 'fair' (l. 4) — an apparently beautiful baby — to the poet she is merely 'perfectly acceptable' (l. 5). It is impossible for her to cherish this child like her own. The fact that this baby's breath 'will fail to enchant' her (l. 10) implies that she knows what it is like to be enchanted by her own baby's breath.

**Alliteration** is used sometimes to accentuate ideas, such as 'Her hot midnight rage' (l. 8) and 'absolute/Abandonment' (l. 12).

The 'monstrous land' (l. 17) that the baby inhabits while asleep suggests she is having a nightmare. It emphasises that the child will need a familiar figure to comfort her when she wakes up.

The phrase 'milk-familiar comforting' (l. 18) reminds us literally of the breast milk that a mother may use to soothe her child, and also metaphorically of care and concern for someone. Shakespeare gave us the phrase 'the milk of human kindness' in *Macbeth*.

The last line contains **repetition** to bring a sense of finality.

## Imagery

Clarke emphasises how desolate the baby will feel if she wakes up to find a stranger instead of her mother. She does this by comparing the baby's situation to that of others who feel abandoned: a 'lover cold in lonely/Sheets' (ll. 13–14) and a woman newly widowed. Clarke states that it will be even 'worse' (l. 12) for the baby than for the lover or the woman: it will be the most extreme sense of loss Clarke can imagine, perhaps because the baby will not understand *why* she has been abandoned.

**Pause for thought**

Is Clarke hinting that the child herself will suffer pain in the future, like the abandoned lover and the woman who loses her husband?

There is a particularly stark image in lines 14–16. A woman's husband has just died in hospital. On her website, Clarke explains that the 'bleached bone' metaphor describes the dead man's bony shape under a white hospital sheet. It is like a bleached bone lying on the beach.

## Ideas to consider

- For whom does Clarke feel more sympathy, the baby or herself?
- Is the poem more about Clarke's own child than the baby she is looking after?
- Is Clarke's sympathy for the child intensified because she is a mother herself?
- Is Clarke sympathising with the child in advance, for tragedies in her life that are yet to come?

# 'Mali'

## What happens?

On her granddaughter's third birthday, Clarke recalls the day that the child was born. Clarke and her daughter had been picking blackberries when her daughter went into premature labour, so Clarke drove her through country lanes to the hospital 20 miles away. The birth was 'easy' and all was well. The following day, the tiny child was brought to the beach and Clarke remembers her instinctive love for Mali being almost overwhelming. Now, three years on, Mali's birthday is celebrated in the garden.

## Structure

The poem consists of four seven-line stanzas. The lines vary between five and twelve syllables.

## Language

The poem is written in the **first person**: it is almost autobiographical.

It is interesting that the whole of the poem takes place outdoors, surrounded by **nature**. (We understand that the birth takes place in a hospital, presumably in a town, but we are given no details.) The setting is the countryside and the beach. (**Enjambement** is used to highlight the rural feel, 'the lazy swish of a dairy herd/rocking so slowly home' (ll. 6–7), where the long, slow phrase echoes the slow movement of the cows.)

We are gradually given clues in stanzas 1 and 2 that enable us to piece together the events on the day of Mali's birth. It is a Sunday (l. 5) in 'late summer' (l. 9). Clarke and her pregnant daughter are picking blackberries, which make their 'fingers purple' (l. 12). The daughter goes into labour prematurely, 'too soon', and she is 'in the wrong place' (l. 14): she had not planned to be staying with her mother for the birth. Clarke drives her daughter to the hospital through 'twenty miles of summer lanes' (l. 4). The journey is made slower because a herd of dairy cows block the road at one point (ll. 6–7). Despite these circumstances the child is born easily (l. 13).

It is **harvest** time. There is emphasis on the profusion of nature — 'apples reddening on heavy trees,/the lanes sweet with brambles' (ll. 10–11). There is a clear link between the fruits of the harvest and the 'fruit' or 'harvest' from a woman — a baby. Clarke stresses the link in lines 15–16: 'things seasonal' (the fruit) 'and out of season' (the premature baby) 'towed home a harvest moon'. It is as if the fruit and the child brought the moon to gaze upon them.

For Mali's birthday party, her grandmother bakes her a cake and hangs 'balloons and streamers' in the trees which make them appear to 'blossom' (ll. 23–24). Like Mali herself, the blossom is out of season.

The last few lines are confusing. Did the people at Mali's party drink the 'cold blue ocean' (l. 26)? Perhaps the grown-ups drank crisp, cold wine that reminded Clarke of the sea. Why are there 'three drops' of blood? Perhaps this is a reference to Mali's age, or to the three generations of women there: Clarke, her daughter and her granddaughter.

## Imagery

The **sea** has an important presence in the poem, which begins with a teasing reference to 'that unmistakable brim and tug of the tide' (l. 2). The image is not fully explained until later, when Clarke knows she is 'hooked again' (l. 20). She uses a fishing metaphor to illustrate the instinctive love she feels for her granddaughter. The 'tide' of love has drawn her to Mali — the natural movement of the sea is a metaphor for the natural instincts of motherhood. The statement that 'Even the sea could not draw me from her' (l. 21) emphasises the extent of her love for her granddaughter.

**Pause for thought**

Do you think Clarke intended us to overlook the harsher connotations of 'hooked' and 'life-sentenced', or did she want to imply something more sinister about maternal love?

Clarke describes her instinctive love for Mali in striking **metaphors**. As well as 'I'm hooked again' — which is not an altogether positive image because a hooked fish dies — Clarke says she is 'life-sentenced' (l. 20). This implies that she is attached to her new granddaughter for the duration of both their lives, but it also has associations with a prison sentence and punishment.

This poem is one in a sequence called *Blood*. 'Blood' is the last word of the poem. We associate blood with the blood of family ties, giving birth, menstruation and the fertility of women. On her website, Clarke points out that an average menstrual cycle of 28 days is the same length as the cycle of the tide, controlled by the moon. Perhaps the 'last blood' refers to Clarke's own very last menstrual cycle: her own fertility is passing as her daughter's is at its height. (Clarke mentions, poignantly, that a woman never knows when her own 'last blood' will be.)

## Ideas to consider

- The birth of a child and the harvest are both seen as products of nature. Nature is bountiful and generous.
- The love of a mother and a grandmother is natural, spontaneous and as irrepressible as the tides.

# 'A Difficult Birth, Easter 1998'

## What happens?

It is Good Friday, the day Christians remember the death of Jesus on the cross. While Clarke and her husband are preparing to celebrate the success of the Irish peace deal (see 'Context', pages 6–8), they realise that an old ewe is about to give birth for the first time. The ewe is in labour while the peace negotiators 'slog it out' (l. 9) to finalise the deal. There is a problem — the lamb seems stuck. Clarke's husband goes for professional help while Clarke stays with the ewe and assists it, easing the lamb out. The second lamb is then born easily. Clarke reflects on the coincidence of three life-affirming events occurring simultaneously: the birth of the lambs, the signing of the peace deal, and the rising of Jesus from the dead.

### Glossary

**ram** *(l. 2)* a male sheep
**barren** *(l. 2)* infertile, unable to have lambs
**hoofing** *(l. 4)* pawing at the straw, making a nest
**Easter 1916** *(l. 10)* see 'Context'
**whitecoats** *(l. 15)* doctors, medical professionals

## Structure

The poem consists of four stanzas, each of six lines. Each line is of similar length, except the final one, which is much shorter. This has the effect both of surprising us — as the three miracle events surprised the observers — and of allowing us space to consider the miracles.

The gap between stanzas 2 and 3 is dramatic: we are made to pause at a crucial moment in the birth — what will happen?

## Language

The poem is written in the **first person**. 'We' is mentioned in stanza 1 and 'you' in line 13. We can assume from the context that Clarke's companion is her husband, even though he is not referred to specifically. The 'We' and 'us' in the final stanza, however, refer to Clarke and the ewe. The **personal pronouns** emphasise the closeness Clarke feels to the ewe. She too has experienced childbirth.

There is a **connection** between the ewe giving birth for the first time and Clarke's own experience of giving birth. Clarke sees them as two females 'together' (l. 19). Perhaps this is why she is able to help the ewe in such an intimate and instinctive way. She is able to ease her own fingers into the ewe to pull the lamb out. It is significant that

 **Pause for thought**

Do you think Clarke believes the 'whitecoats' really do 'know best'?

in the end the ewe has no need of a vet. Maybe Clarke is implying that women have less need of 'whitecoats' (l. 15) (the medical professionals in a maternity ward) than we think.

The birth of the first lamb is described very physically. Clarke and the ewe 'strain' (l. 19) and the ewe's limbs 'creak' (l. 20). The ewe is exhausted and 'famished' (l. 21) after the birth.

## Imagery

Although it apparently focuses on the unexpected birth of the lambs, the poem keeps the three narratives in parallel throughout the poem.

The ewe's waters are described by the **metaphor** 'lost salty ocean' (l. 8). The liquid in the amniotic sac, protecting the young in the womb, is salty. Perhaps 'ocean' reminds us of the dangerous journey the lamb is undertaking (as though on a small boat).

Picturedisc

However, the birth of the second lamb is easy: it 'slips through her opened door' (l. 23). The difficult birth of the first lamb has opened the birth canal for the second. Perhaps this metaphor suggests that the hardest stage of any process is the first one.

## Ideas to consider

* The poem is about three miracles: the rising of Christ from the dead, the signing of the Irish peace deal and the birth of twin lambs to an elderly ewe. Each of these events was unexpected and, in each case, life seems to have triumphed over death.
* What is Clarke's attitude to medical intervention during birth?
* Do you think Clarke believes that the first stage of the peace process and the first stage of Jesus' resurrection were also the hardest parts?

## Pause for thought

Do you feel that Clarke believes any one of these miracles to be any more important than the others, or are they all of equal value to her?

# 'The Field-Mouse'

## What happens?

The poet remembers a hot summer's day at haymaking time. The rural peace is destroyed by fighter planes training to take part in the war in Bosnia. When a child comes crying because a mouse has been injured by the mower, Clarke is reminded of the injuries and deaths going on elsewhere in Europe in the war. Rather than celebrate a successful haymaking, she grieves for the other tiny creatures killed during the mowing and for those who have taken refuge in the garden (like refugees in wartime). That night, thinking of the animals caught up in haymaking, she dreams of the innocent children caught up in the conflict in Bosnia.

### Glossary

**snare drum** (l. 1) a drum with wires stretched across one surface, to produce a rattling sound

**lime** (l. 8) ground up limestone, used as a fertiliser

## Structure

The poem consists of three stanzas of nine lines. The lengths of the lines vary, perhaps to suggest that life is unpredictable.

## Language

Clarke writes in the **present tense** even though she is describing a day in the past. As well as making the poem more dramatic, the tense is significant because it reminds us of all the violence happening now, today.

The poem is written in the **first person**. Other people feature, but remain **anonymous**: those cutting the hay, 'our neighbour' (l. 7) and 'The child' (l. 10). This links to the anonymous people involved in the war — those flying the jets and firing guns, and those injured and killed.

The poem is full of **contrasts** between Wales and Bosnia, peace and war. Yet it is disturbing that the war happening hundreds of miles away is felt on Clarke's farm. 'The air hums with jets' (l. 2) practising for war, and the radio tells 'terrible news' (l. 4).

### Key point

In the Bosnian conflict, neighbours turned against each other (despite past friendships), as religious conflict grew.

The links between Wales and Bosnia are developed in stanza 2. Both countries are part of 'Europe' (l. 16) and death is everywhere. The child comes through 'killed flowers' (l. 10) with a dying mouse and Clarke uses brutal language: 'finish it off' (l. 13). Clarke feels guilty and responsible, 'staring at what we have crushed' (l. 18). On her website, Clarke points out that the literal translation of 'cutting the hay' in Welsh is 'killing the hay'.

The third stanza describes the 'saved' (l. 20) animals, the ones that escaped the mower. We are reminded of the human refugees in the Bosnian war, even though Clarke cannot bear to read the facts about them in the newspapers (l. 23).

Clarke uses her neighbour to illustrate a final contrast between her life in rural Wales and the lives of those in Bosnia. In the first stanza he is ploughing lime into his land. This provides the Clarkes' land with 'a chance gift of sweetness' (l. 9), as some of the lime is carried by the breeze over the hedge. However, in the final lines of the poem she imagines him as a 'stranger', throwing stones over the hedge like missiles, 'wounding my land'.

## Imagery

The opening **metaphor**, 'the long grass is a snare drum', vividly describes the noise of the insects in the grass. It lulls us into a false sense of security. We think that the poem will describe a beautiful rural scene, but the second line surprises us with 'The air hums with jets.' Clarke challenges our expectations: the jets themselves, we suddenly realise, sound like insects.

The field is **personified**: it is 'hurt' (l. 16), as if it feels the pain of the animals that die. Later, we hear, 'the field lies bleeding' (l. 19), and we are reminded of the battle*fields* of Bosnia.

In Clarke's nightmare vision, she uses a **simile** to link the children to the mice: 'their bones brittle as mouse-ribs'. She knows that children in a real war are as fragile and vulnerable as the creatures in the hay field.

## Ideas to consider

* The poem is about the ways in which man inflicts harm on others.
* We are reminded of the fragility of all life — human and animal. The mouse is a symbol of the very weakest.
* Do you think that the children who are horrified by the death of the mouse symbolise children all over the world who are horrified by the suffering caused by the war?
* Does the poem contain any hope?

# 'October'

## What happens?

Clarke describes the funeral of a close friend, one October day. (The friend's name was Frances Horovitz and she was the same age as Clarke.) Clarke sets a sombre tone in the first stanza, focusing on the grey weather and the autumnal plants losing their leaves, before describing the burial itself. Her friend's death reminds Clarke of her own mortality. She feels a compulsion to write as much as she can, as fast as she can, before her own death. She feels the significance that each year she passes the calendar day on which she will die, without knowing which day it is.

### Glossary

**poplars** (l. 1) trees with straight trunks and large leaves

**lobelia** (l. 5) trailing plant with tiny blue, white or pink flowers (here, blue)

**Orcop** (l. 7) a village in England, close to the Welsh border

## Structure

The poem consists of three stanzas, two of six lines and the final one of eight lines. The lines are mainly iambic. Stanzas 2 and 3 merge into each other; 'fall of flowers' (l. 12) and 'Over the page the pen' (l. 13) combine to make one iambic line.

## Language

The poem is written in the **first person** and we realise that stanzas 2 and 3 are acutely personal to Clarke.

Stanza 1 contains words relating to **darkness** and **death**: 'broken', 'dead', 'darkens', 'dreadlocks', 'tangled', 'brown'. This sets a depressing, reflective tone, appropriate for a poem about a dead friend. The wind in the poplars would be noisy.

The face of the lion darkens in the shower because wet stone is darker than dry, but perhaps there is also a suggestion that the lion's mood 'darkens'. The lion must have had lobelia planted on top of (or near to) its head, creating 'dreadlocks' (l . 5). Now, the once-blue flowers hanging around its face are turning 'brown'.

The language describing the funeral is **stark** and pared down (so it is not even grammatically correct English): 'My friend dead and the graveyard at Orcop' (l. 7). Perhaps this is in order to suggest both the finality of death and the fragility of Clarke's emotions. It is raining and the people are crying, so the tears and rain get mixed up on people's faces — 'rain, weeping in the air' (l. 10).

There is a **contrast** between 'the slow/fall of flowers' (ll. 11–12) in stanza 2 and the pen rushing along at the start of stanza 3. This shows how Clarke has suddenly been galvanised into writing, so as not to waste the life she has left. Another contrast is present in 'health feels like pain' (l. 14), which suggests Clarke feels guilty about being alive and well.

The **punctuation** in the final stanza (ll. 14–17) helps to suggest speed as Clarke rushes to get everything written. Perhaps these lines refer to some of the subjects that she wants to make into poems. She uses an **imperative verb**, 'must' (l. 18), to show how determined she is to make the most of the time until her own 'death-day' (l. 19).

## Imagery

One of the branches in the poplar tree is broken, 'a dead arm in the bright trees' (l. 2). Perhaps this branch represents Clarke's dead friend, while she and the other people they knew are still alive and 'bright', like the trees. The leaves on the trees are turning to 'gold' (l. 3): it is interesting that they are at their most beautiful as they are dying.

Clarke uses **similes** in the second stanza, first to show the slightness of her friend's coffin, 'lighter/than hare-bones on men's shoulders' (ll. 8–9), and then to show 'The grave/deep as a well' (l. 11). The **enjambement** between 'grave' and 'deep' helps to illustrate its plunging depth. It is interesting that a well provides water, vital for life.

Another simile is used in the final stanza: 'the pen/runs faster than wind's white steps over grass' (ll. 12–13). This describes beautifully how grass catches the sunlight and flashes white when it is flattened by the wind. The **alliteration** gives a sense of speed.

Clarke compares herself to an animal in the final lines of the poem, escaping from a predator — death. (Perhaps she is imagining herself as a hare, linking to the 'hare-bones' simile.) In this **metaphor**, she is 'winning ground' (l. 19) — getting further away from what is out to get her.

### Pause for thought

The well image could fit within the poem in two ways:

1 The body is being returned to a well, so what once had life is being returned to the source of life — the body has gone full circle.

2 The body will blend with the water that will be drunk by other people, so the dead woman will feed the living.

Which version fits your reading of the poem better?

## Ideas to consider

- It is significant that Clarke's friend died in autumn, at the time of year when leaves and plants are dying. How do you think Clarke may have responded had her friend died during another season?
- Is Clarke *triumphant* at the end when she claims she is 'winning ground', or merely *relieved* that she is still alive?
- Our 'death-day' is the opposite of our birthday.

# 'On the Train'

## What happens?

Clarke describes a homeward train journey she makes early one morning. It is so early that she expects her husband is still in bed and so does not phone him; she listens to her Walkman radio instead. She lists other people's early-morning activities: they listen to their radios as they drop children off at school and drive to the station to catch their commuter trains to work. A disturbing note comes at the end of the second stanza: an earlier train has crashed and become a 'blazing bone-ship' (l. 12).

In the third stanza Clarke imagines the loved ones of those in the crash desperately trying to reach them on mobile phones. She imagines their distraught reactions when the phones go unanswered. When Clarke then phones home herself there is no answer, and she becomes anxious. She needs to hear a familiar voice and so, today, she is 'tolerant/of mobiles' (ll. 22–23). The cliché 'Darling, I'm on the train' (l. 24) is, for once, necessary.

## Structure

The poem consists of four stanzas of six lines. The second stanza is one long sentence, illustrating the seamless pattern of people's morning routines.

## Language

The poem is written in the **first person**. We assume that 'you' (l. 5) is Clarke's husband, but she does not give more details, perhaps so that the poem can be more universal and speak for the feelings of many.

It is interesting that the first word of the poem is 'Cradled'. The train that Clarke is travelling on rocks like a cradle, and we associate cradles with warmth and security — so it is **ironic** that Clarke goes on to describe a dangerous crash. 'Cradled' also links to 'dreaming' (l. 12)

The poem contains **repetition**, such as 'rocking, rocking the rails' (l. 2) and 'I'm thinking of you.../thinking of me' (ll. 5–6). The repetition mimics the clickety-clack sound of the train and perhaps also the repetition we experience in the sameness of our daily lives. Later on in the poem, however, the repetition highlights how, for some, daily life will not be the same again: 'Please call later. And calling later,/calling later

### Key point

The poem was written about the Paddington train crash on 5 October 1999, when two trains collided. Thirty-one people died and 400 were injured.

On her website Clarke states that she wrote the poem as she heard the crash being reported on Radio 4, while she was travelling home from Manchester to Wales.

their phones ring' (ll. 15–16). The train is reduced to 'rubble' (l. 16), just as people's lives are reduced to 'rubble' (l. 17) by losing a loved one in the crash.

It is interesting that Clarke refers to her Walkman as a 'black box' (l. 3). We think of black box flight recorders that record an air pilot's words and movements, and are used following an accident to piece together what happened. Perhaps she is giving us a clue that a tragedy is about to take place.

In the second stanza there is a **contrast** between the trains that gently 'slide out of stations…/dreaming' (ll. 11–12) and the violent, ugly, vivid picture of one train as 'the blazing bone-ship'.

The poem contains many references to different **sounds**: the rhythm of the train, the radio, 'locks click' (l. 10). The third stanza in particular is full of sound. We hear the Vodaphone recorded message, phones ringing and the disturbing 'howl' (l. 18) of the bereaved.

In the final stanza, Clarke uses **short phrases** ('I phone. No answer': l. 19) and **imperatives** ('talk to me…/Pick up the phone': ll. 21–22) to indicate her anxiety. People using mobile phones have acquired the reputation of saying the apparently unnecessary phrase, 'I'm on the train.' On the day of an accident, however, that message is the one phrase that the friends and relatives of train passengers yearn to hear, to know that their loved one is not involved in the tragedy.

**Pause for thought**

The poem refers to modern technology which we do not usually consider as 'poetic', yet it is also full of love, which is a 'poetic' subject.

## Imagery

Clarke uses a metaphor to describe the crashed train as 'the blazing bone-ship' (l. 12). On her website Clarke notes: 'I was thinking of the burning funeral ships the Celts used to push out to sea, containing the bodies of their heroes. I wanted to suggest something noble, tragic, heroic, because real people would be grieving, and deserved no less than the dignity of the noblest image I could conjure.'

There is a distressing image of the 'wolves [who] howl into silent telephones' (l. 18). This would be almost comic in a different context. Here it conveys the raw sound of grieving and the horrifying change that has come over these people; their lives have been transformed in a savage way.

## Ideas to consider

* Who is Clarke referring to in 'Let them say it' (l. 23)? Does she mean anyone who uses a mobile phone? Those on the train with her? The dead?
* The poem makes us consider how many of our habitual activities (like taking the train to work) may end in our death. Nothing is guaranteed; no one can see into the future.

# 'Cold Knap Lake'

## What happens?

Clarke describes a day when she watched a crowd pull an apparently drowned child from a lake. (On her website, she says that she was about six. Perhaps she was the same age as the child.) Clarke's mother gave the child mouth-to-mouth resuscitation and saved her life. Clarke's father then took the child back to her 'poor' (l. 13) home, where she was punished for having almost drowned.

As Clarke reflects on the dramatic events, she thinks about memory. It can become infused with other influences, like stories and the imagination, to create new 'truths' (see 'Ideas to consider').

## Structure

The poem consists of five stanzas of varying numbers of lines and varying line lengths. There is some **half-rhyme** within each stanza (such as 'earth'/'breath', 'bowed'/'soaked' and 'silent'/'it' in stanza 2) and a rhyming couplet to conclude. The half-rhymes set up echoes within the poem, which add to the magical, fairy-tale theme.

## Language

The poem is written in the **first person**. It is not immediately clear who 'We' (l. 1) refers to, but we come to realise that Clarke is talking about herself as a child with her mother and father. It is set in wartime or just afterwards. The language used, 'frock' (l. 7) and 'poor house' (l. 13), adds to the period feel.

There is a **sense of drama** in the narrative of the poem. We assume that the child has 'drowned' (l. 2), which is confirmed by 'she lay for dead' (l. 4), yet she is miraculously brought to life again. We hear about the 'heroine' (l. 6) before we are told that she is Clarke's 'mother' (l. 8). Like a good storyteller, Clarke keeps us guessing. The **alliteration** in 'drawn by the dread of it' (l. 10) heightens the tension further.

### Key point

Cold Knap Lake is an artificial lake in Barry, south Wales. On her website, Clarke comments that the name of the lake is haunting because of the word 'cold'.

**Colour** is used in an interesting way in the poem. The child is at first swathed in 'green silk' and is 'blue-lipped' (l. 3). When revived, she is 'rosy' (l. 12), perhaps as if she has taken on some of the 'red' (l. 6) of Clarke's mother.

**Swans** are not mentioned in the first part of the poem, but are introduced when Clarke imagines what might have been. Maybe there really were swans on the lake that day, or maybe Clarke's childhood imagination added them to the scene. Swans often feature in traditional fairy tales, where they have a magical or mystical role. Either way, they are a vague, shadowy presence in the poem.

Lines 16–20 make up one sentence. It is hard to read: there is hardly any punctuation and the words do not make complete grammatical sense. We feel disoriented and uncertain, as Clarke does when she remembers the day.

## Imagery

Clarke describes the waterweed clinging to the half-drowned child as 'silk' (l. 3) that 'dressed' her. It is interesting that she has made something threatening sound so beautiful. The weed *could* have dragged the child further underwater, but Clarke makes the weed into a garment fit for a princess in a fairy tale.

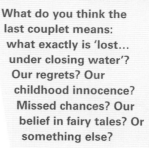

**Pause for thought**

What do you think the last couplet means: what exactly is 'lost… under closing water'? Our regrets? Our childhood innocence? Missed chances? Our belief in fairy tales? Or something else?

When the child is revived, she is 'bleating' (l. 11) like a lamb. Perhaps Clarke wants us to associate the girl rising from the dead with Christ, who also rose from the dead and was portrayed as a lamb.

As in the first stanza, the imagery in the fourth stanza *seems* beautiful, but is actually threatening. The willows are **personified**: they have 'dipped [their] fingers' into the water (l. 17), perhaps to grab the child. The mud 'blooms' like a flower (l. 18), but it obscures things. The swans are referred to as 'heavy' (l. 19) and their wings 'beat and whistle' (l. 20) — descriptions that are at odds with the usual image of swans as graceful white birds.

## Ideas to consider

* Compare the reaction of the child's parents to the reaction of Clarke's parents.
* In the poem, a relatively vivid memory of a real-life event becomes a vaguer memory that is infused with fairy tales. It is sometimes hard to be sure whether our childhood memories are memories of real events or whether they have been influenced by other things (such as what people have told us, or stories or pictures that we have seen). Clarke illustrates this blurring of the truth in the stanza beginning 'Was I there?' (l. 15). The question highlights her lack of certainty about what really happened. Perhaps Clarke is asking us to question how accurate any of our childhood memories are.
* It is interesting that the final couplet seems tragic: it speaks of 'All lost things' (l. 21) under the water with 'the poor man's daughter'. Yet we know that the poor man's daughter was saved and is *not* now under the water. Perhaps Clarke is imagining what could have been the case — what would have happened if it really was a fairy tale.

# Poem by poem
# Pre-1914
# Poetry Bank

## Biographies

**William Blake** (1757–1827) was the son of a London hosier. Instead of going to school, Blake was apprenticed to an engraver, learning how to illustrate books. He then studied at the Royal Academy of Arts. He married Catherine when he was 25; they had no children. He developed an interest in mysticism and, encouraged by visionary religious friends, began to publish poetry. In 1784 he set up his own print shop and began to publish his own works, including *Songs of Innocence and of Experience*. His work was only partially appreciated during his lifetime: he was thought of as gifted but mad.

**Robert Browning** (1812–89) was brought up by his sister in London and was mainly self-educated, roaming through his father's large library. He dropped out of university. He travelled in Europe and began to publish poetry (anonymously at first) and plays. In 1846 he famously eloped to Italy with the poet Elizabeth Barrett; they lived there until she died 15 years later. He set many of his poems in Europe. By the time he returned to England he was a famous and successful writer.

**John Clare** (1793–1864) was a rural labourer's son from Northamptonshire and grew up to be a hedge-setter. He always loved the countryside and was inspired to write about it, publishing his first

Robert Browning

poems in 1820. He married Martha Turner in the same year but never really got over his first love, Mary Joyce. His sadness overcame him and he was admitted to an asylum for the insane in 1837. Four years later he escaped and walked back to Mary, believing she was his wife. The rest of his life was spent in the asylum, writing poetry. He always insisted upon using his own language, dialect and grammar.

**Oliver Goldsmith** (1730–74) was born and brought up in Ireland, the son of a clergyman. His application to join the priesthood was turned down, so he turned to medicine, setting himself up as a physician without gaining a degree. He then began writing reviews for periodicals (literary magazines) and published more and more of his own works, although he never made much money. He also wrote plays, including the comic *She Stoops to Conquer*, which was a great success. He never married.

**Thomas Hardy** (1840–1928) was the son of a stonemason, and was encouraged by his mother to read throughout his childhood. He became an architect and worked in London, but continued to read voraciously and soon began to write his own novels. The success of his fourth published novel, *Far From the Madding Crowd*, in 1874, enabled him to give up architecture for writing and to marry Emma Gifford. Later on he gave up writing novels and turned to poetry, but continued to focus on the suffering in the world and the ironies of life. He married Florence Dugdale 2 years after Emma's death, when he was 74 and a famous writer.

**Gerard Manley Hopkins** (1844–89) grew up in Essex, the eldest of nine children. He won a scholarship to Oxford University and there became interested in exploring religion. He converted to Roman Catholicism and later joined the more extreme Jesuit organisation to train as a priest. At this stage he burned all his poems, believing that he could not serve God and write poetry at the same time. He only returned to writing in 1875, after an interval of 8 years. He tried to glorify God through his poetry, but he found life as a parish priest hard. Soon after a spell in Glasgow (where he wrote 'Inversnaid') he left the priesthood to become a professor at Dublin University. He died of typhoid.

**Ben Jonson** (1572/3–1637) never saw his own father, who died before he was born. He had an exciting early life, including fighting as a soldier in Flanders (where he killed an enemy champion in single combat). He also acted in a company of travelling players, where he killed a fellow actor in a duel and was subsequently imprisoned. He wrote many plays for the court (the first of which included Shakespeare in the cast), and poetry. James I admired his work and gave him a pension, which was a great honour. He was also given an honorary degree by Oxford University.

**William Shakespeare** (1564–1616) spent his childhood in Stratford-upon-Avon, where his father was a prominent local merchant. William probably attended the local grammar school. He married Anne Hathaway, who was 8 years his senior, and they had three children. It is not known when he began to write plays, but he was a member of the successful troupe The Lord Chamberlain's Men, which developed into London's leading company, based at the Globe Theatre. His sonnets were published in 1609; his many plays were not printed during his lifetime, simply performed. It was not until seven years after Shakespeare's death that the plays were first published.

Alfred Tennyson

**Alfred Tennyson** (1809–92) was the son of a rural priest. He went to Cambridge University and there wrote much poetry, even winning a prize. He travelled to Europe with his close friend Arthur Hallam, but Hallam drowned in 1833 and Tennyson wrote his famous poem 'In Memoriam' in his memory. His often melancholic and lyrical poetry became popular, and Queen Victoria made him poet laureate in 1850 (the same year in which he married) and, later, a baronet.

**Chidiock (Charles) Tichborne** (1558–86) was brought up in a Roman Catholic family. The Protestant Elizabeth I (having been excommunicated by the Pope) made Catholicism illegal, and Tichborne conspired in a Catholic plot to kill her. He was discovered and was executed by hanging. He was also disembowelled while still alive; when Elizabeth heard of this, she was so shocked that she banned the practice immediately. The 'Elegy' he wrote to his wife on the eve of his death is his only surviving poem. The *Anthology* is mistaken over his name: he was baptised Chidiock, not Charles.

**Walt Whitman** (1819–92) was born and brought up in New York. He received little schooling and worked, among other things, as a printer, politician and teacher. He travelled around America and contributed to various magazines while writing poetry. His work became widely admired. During the Civil War (1861–65) he volunteered as a hospital visitor; he later lived quietly in New Jersey. He never married and was probably homosexual.

**William Wordsworth** (1770–1850) was brought up in Cumbria, but his mother died when he was only 8 years old and his father when he was 13. He left Cambridge University to tour Europe and spent a period in Paris, where he supported the ideals of the French Revolution. He met the poet Coleridge in 1795; together they published *Lyrical Ballads*, a collection celebrating nature and self-expression that inspired other Romantic writers. Wordsworth married in 1802 and had five children, but he remained close to his sister, Dorothy. He settled in the Lake District and wrote much long, narrative poetry that proved popular. He became poet laureate in 1843.

**William Butler Yeats** (1865–1939), born in Ireland, was the eldest son of a famous painter. He himself began to study art, but gave it up in favour of literature, editing the work of other poets and writing his own. He was a committed Republican and supported movements to make Ireland independent from Britain — a theme that occurs in much of his poetry. He loved the beautiful and politically active Maud Gonne, but she refused him. He later married Georgie Hyde-Lees, a mystic, whose 'communicators' influenced his work. Yeats continued to be active in Irish politics throughout his life, becoming a senator in 1922. He was awarded the Nobel prize for literature in 1923.

TopFoto

W. B. Yeats

# 'On my first Sonne'

## What happens?

The poet is mourning the death of his dearly loved seven-year-old son. Ironically, he blames himself for the child's death: his 'sinne' (l. 2), or sin, was to have loved him too much. He considers a paradox: we mourn when we ought to rejoice that someone has escaped the burdens of the world and gone to Heaven. He resolves at the end never to love so intensely again, in order to avoid the same loss and grief.

### Glossary

**tho'wert** (l. 3) thou wert, or you were

**scap'd** (l. 7) escaped

**hence-forth** (l. 11) from now on

## Structure

The poem consists of six pairs of **rhyming couplets**. Most of the lines are **end-stopped**, so the rhymes chime softly through the poem. The lines are **iambic pentameters**, so there is a slow, even, natural rhythm.

## Language and imagery

Jonson writes in the **first person** to express his own personal emotions. The poem is spoken to the child, from father to son, and consequently feels very intimate.

The child was his 'right hand' (l. 1) because he was the eldest son (Jonson's heir) and because Jesus sat at God's right hand.

Jonson uses **banking imagery**. He says his son was 'lent' (l. 3) to him and that he, Jonson, paid back his creditor 'on the just day' (l. 4). As a Christian, Jonson believes that God creates all people, and he knows that he could never have expected to *own* something as precious as his son. He has returned him to God.

Jonson asks **rhetorical questions**. He wonders why he should 'lament' (l. 6) death when he really should 'envie' (l. 6) his son for going to a better place, i.e. Heaven. The world is full of 'fleshes rage' (l. 7) and 'miserie' (l. 8), while his son is able to 'Rest in soft peace' (l. 9).

**Pause for thought**

**How do you think Jonson saw God?**

The word 'poetry' comes from a Greek word meaning 'a thing made or created'. So Jonson — a writer more famous than Shakespeare in his day — is saying that his son is 'his best piece of poetrie' (l. 10), the best thing he ever created.

### Ideas to consider

* God is portrayed as a banker who lends humans to the world for a specified time. Likening birth and death to business transactions may sound callous, but Jonson seems in no doubt that his son really is in 'soft peace' with God, and is comforted by the thought.
* There is an interesting tension in the poem. If God 'lent' the child to Jonson, God must have been his creator. Yet Jonson also claims to have created the child, in the 'poetrie' image.

## 'The Song of the Old Mother'

### What happens?

As the Old Mother works from dawn to dusk she compares herself to rich and idle people. She has to do all the cleaning and cooking, while the young girls lie in bed all day and only worry if the wind disturbs their beautifully arranged hair. The old woman is tired and lonely and appears to resent her work.

**Glossary**

tress *(l. 8)* a portion or lock of hair

### Structure

The poem is composed of five **rhyming couplets**, and so is a 'Song' — but not a very cheerful one. It is made up of one complete sentence, perhaps to suggest the never-ending nature of the woman's work. There are ten syllables in each line and ten lines in the poem, so it is a bit like a square, ten by ten. Perhaps this reflects the rigidity of her day.

## Language and imagery

The poem is written in the **first person**. Yeats takes on the **persona** of the old woman.

It is clear that the old woman works all day long, from 'dawn' (l. 1) 'Till stars are beginning to blink and peep' (l. 4). The stars are **personified** — although we don't get the impression that they peep down at her with any sympathy.

Her work is described in **bald**, **simple verbs**: 'kneel', 'blow', 'scrub', 'bake', 'sweep' (ll. 1–3). There is also the **imperative** 'must' (ll. 3 and 9). The verbs emphasise the harshness of her life.

In **contrast**, the young 'lie long and dream' (l. 5). The **alliteration** lengthens the 'l' sound, suggesting that they languish in idleness. There are strong comparisons between the old poor woman and the young rich girls. The young have nothing to do; the Old Mother 'must work' (l. 9).

Perhaps the most important of the old woman's tasks is to tend the fire. It is an effort: she has to 'kneel' to coax the 'seed' to life (l. 2). At the end of the day that 'seed' becomes 'feeble and cold' (l. 10). The dying fire is a **metaphor** for the old woman's life. She too is becoming 'feeble and cold', but the sad thing is that nobody seems to realise or care.

## Ideas to consider

- The title of the poem states that the woman is a 'Mother', yet it is unlikely that the 'young' are her own children. Perhaps her own offspring have grown up and left her all alone. Perhaps they have died. Or perhaps she is not a mother at all, but has somehow acquired the title 'Mother'. (If so, is that respectful or disrespectful?)

**Pause for thought**

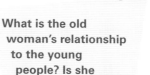

What is the old woman's relationship to the young people? Is she their servant?

# 'The Affliction of Margaret'

## What happens?

The poem is about the desperation of a mother to find news of her son, her 'only child' (l. 9), whom she has not heard from for seven years. She describes his happy childhood and how proud she was of him when he left home. Discounting the idea that he may simply be neglecting her, she worries about what may have happened to him — he could be ashamed to come home because he is impoverished, or he

**Glossary**

**affliction** pain, misery

**beguiled** *(l. 11)* deluded, cheated

**beauteous to behold** *(l. 16)* beautiful to look at

**intercourse** *(l. 59)* communication

could even be imprisoned or drowned. If he is dead, she reasons that there cannot be communication between the living and dead, or she would have heard from him. Finally the poem goes full circle and ends as it began, with a plea for news of the son.

## Structure

The poem consists of eleven equal stanzas of seven lines. There is a strict **rhyme scheme** of ABABCCC in each one. The rhymes in the last three lines are often extremely poignant. (Look again at stanzas 4, 7 and 11.)

## Language and imagery

The poem is written in the **first person**: Wordsworth is taking on the **persona** of Margaret. It is interesting that we know *her* name but never learn the name of the son.

Margaret uses fairly formal language, which suggests she is educated. She uses the familiar 'thou' instead of 'you' (like the French 'tu'), as was usual 200 years ago.

### Pause for thought

Is Margaret's impression of her son accurate, or is she deceiving herself (and us)?

Margaret has numerous ideas about why she has not heard from her son, ranging from simple 'Neglect' (l. 29) to fears that he's been 'summon'd to the Deep' (l. 54) or has died in some other way.

The seventh stanza (ll. 43–49) contains the most complex language and imagery. The 'fowls of Heaven' are birds. Margaret is saying that birds can fly far and wide, aided by the winds ('blasts of Heaven'); *because* they can fly they can quickly find their 'delight' — or whatever it is they are searching for. In contrast, humans are tied down to 'land and sea' and so do not have the freedom of birds. Therefore all Margaret can do is wish for her son to come home and pray that he is comforted, wherever he is — although she recognises this is a 'vain' hope. The stanza expresses how frustrated Margaret feels that she is powerless to find her son.

'The very shadows of the clouds
Have power to shake me as they pass'

## Ideas to consider

* There is a sense of mystery about Margaret's son. The reader doesn't know his fate; we are left to speculate, like Margaret.
* Margaret is clearly proud of her son: 'He was among the prime in worth' (l. 15). How much can we believe her claims?

# 'The Little Boy Lost'/'The Little Boy Found'

## What happens?

In the first of this pair of poems a child wanders alone on a dark night through dangerous boggy ground. He seems to be abandoned by his father. In the second poem a lost child is returned by God to his distraught mother. (We assume that it is the same child.)

## Structure

Each poem is composed of two **quatrains**, and both rhyme ABCB. They seem like nursery rhymes — on the surface.

## Language and imagery

The first poem begins in the **first person** as we hear the boy's pleas to his father not to abandon him. This plunges the reader straight into a dramatic and dangerous situation and we sympathise with the boy, although we are not sure whether the father has deliberately abandoned the child or whether the boy has simply wandered away. Blake then switches to the **third person**: we are told what happens by an omniscient (all-knowing) narrator.

There is a mysterious reference to 'vapour' (LBL, l. 8). Perhaps the child was lost in the mist — or was he following it (as Blake suggests in the engraving illustrating the poem)? The second poem seems to confirm this: the child is 'Led by the wand'ring light' (LBF, l. 2), but we are not told exactly what this light is, and whether it is good or evil.

The Little Boy Lost illustration from *Songs of Innocence and of Experience*

## Ideas to consider

* Blake makes us question the role of a father. We are horrified in the first poem when the father abandons his child, and in such a dangerous place. Yet in the second poem God appears in human form, 'like his father' (l. 4), and leads the boy to safety. Christians call God 'Our Father'.

We also consider the role of the mother. She was obviously desperate to find her child, as she is 'in sorrow pale' (LBF, l. 7), but she was looking in the wrong place, 'the lonely dale' (LBF, l. 7). She would not have found him without God's help.

### Key point

Blake was an illustrator, poet and mystic. These poems come from *The Songs of Innocence and of Experience*. Deceptively simple poems, they were written apparently for children, but they have much Christian symbolism and important messages for adults too.

### Pause for thought

What do the child, mother and father represent? What do the 'vapour' and the 'wand'ring light' symbolise? What messages was Blake trying to convey through the poems?

# 'Tichborne's Elegy'

## What happens?

In the poem, Tichborne laments his premature death. He uses a number of comparisons and images to show that his life is wasted and is over too early.

## Structure

The poem consists of three equal stanzas of six lines, each with a **refrain**. There is an ABABCC rhyme scheme and a regular iambic rhythm, which shows remarkable control for someone who was due to die in the morning. Perhaps concentrating on writing an ordered poem helped to keep Tichborne calm.

### Glossary

**cares** *(l. 1)* worries
**tares** *(l. 3)* vetch, a weed in corn
**shade** *(l. 14)* here, a ghost
**glass** *(l. 17)* an hourglass (see the illustration above the poem in the *Anthology*)

## Language and imagery

The poem is, of course, in the **first person**. (It is significant that, of all the poems in the *Anthology*, this one was never meant for publication. It contains Tichborne's intimate thoughts, meant only for his wife.)

Each line is a **balanced statement**. The first half of the line sets up an image; the second, after the **caesura**, shows how that image, in Tichborne's situation, is turned on its head. For example, he should be in his 'prime of youth' but is instead in the winter of his life, with a cold 'frost of cares' (l. 1); the earth he 'trod' is about to be his 'tomb' (l. 15). 'But' is used a lot to mark the contrast and here means 'only'.

## Pause for thought

Which contrasting metaphors do you feel are most effective?

Tichborne uses various **metaphors** to illustrate his state. For instance, the first stanza contains food imagery ('feast of joy … dish of pain': l. 2) and farming imagery ('crop of corn … field of tares': l. 3). This last metaphor is interesting, as Jesus uses a similar image in a parable.

The refrain is a sort of **paradox**: he still lives, but his life is essentially over.

## Ideas to consider

* Tichborne uses 'My' and 'I' frequently. Do you think this shows introspection or selfishness? (He doesn't appear to think of his loved ones at all.)

**Key point**

Tichborne, a Roman Catholic, was sentenced to death for having joined a plot to kill Elizabeth I. He was only 28 years old. On the night before his execution, he wrote to his wife Agnes, enclosing this poem.

# 'The Man He Killed'

## What happens?

The poet tells an unidentified listener about a man he killed. He says that in any other circumstance he and the man would have been friends and shared a drink. Because they met in wartime, they happened to be enemies and shot each other.

### Glossary

**nipperkin** *(l. 4)* a small measure (less than half a pint) for wine, ale, etc.
**ranged** *(l. 5)* arranged (in lines)
**'list** *(l. 13)* enlist, join the army
**traps** *(l. 15)* trappings, possessions, stuff

## Structure

The poem consists of five **quatrains**, each rhyming ABAB. The lines are short (lines 1, 2 and 4 contain six syllables; line 3 has eight) and so the poem appears very simple. Perhaps the deceptively simple form reinforces the simple message.

## Language and imagery

**Key point**

Hardy wrote this poem during the second Boer War (1899–1902). The poem is not just about that war, however — it could be about *any* war.

The poem is written in the **first person**: Hardy takes on the **persona** of the soldier. The poem is written within speech marks, so either the soldier is narrating what happened to

someone else or the speech marks reinforce the fact that this is a persona — not the poet reflecting to himself, but someone talking aloud, relating his experience to an audience (perhaps the listening poet).

The poem starts in the **conditional** tense, 'Had he and I but met' (or '*If* we had met'). We get the feeling that the soldier means 'If only'; right from the start there is an element of doubt.

The first stanza **contrasts** with the second. Instead of sharing a drink together casually, the two soldiers were arranged in formal lines and obliged to shoot each other. The simple, one-syllable words make lines 7–8 bald and stark.

In the third stanza, the soldier searches for a reason *why* he killed his 'foe' (l. 10). The **repetition** of 'because' and the use of 'Just so… of course…/That's clear enough' (ll. 11–12) suggest that he himself is unconvinced. It is **ironic** that he can't explain why the man had to die.

The fourth stanza highlights the similarities between the men. Both enlisted casually, 'Off-hand like' (l. 14), because they were out of work and had sold all their things.

## Ideas to consider

* Why is the soldier telling the tale? Do you think he needs to get it off his chest? Does he feel guilty for killing a fellow who would have been a friend if they had met in any other circumstance (ll.18–20)?
* What is Hardy's attitude to war? Does he really think it is 'quaint and curious' (l. 17), or is that an ironic understatement?

# 'Patrolling Barnegat'

## What happens?

The poem is set on a dark, stormy night. The narrator is walking along the beach alone and he finds it hard to make out exactly what he can see through the wild weather. He wonders if he spies a wreck; we, like the poet, are never sure.

> **Key point**
>
> Barnegat is a beach in New Jersey, USA, in what is today called Ocean County. It is famous for sailing.

## Structure

The poem consists of 14 lines and is therefore a **sonnet**, but a very unusual one. Sonnets are often ordered pieces about love or loss: this one is confused and chaotic. There is only one full stop, right at the end, but even then the poem is not a complete sentence because there is no main verb. It is simply a list of clauses piled together. The lack of order in the poetry echoes the wild scenes it describes.

## Language and imagery

The poem is apparently written in the **first person** but the narrator never refers to himself (or herself) directly. In fact there are no personal pronouns. This both distances the reader from the reporter, making us concentrate on the storm, and alienates us, so *we* feel alone too.

Every line ends with a verb ending in '–ing', a **present participle**. This helps to create pace in the poem as we sense we are being rushed along, and also sets up a mysterious echoing sound-track.

The poet uses **personification** to create an atmosphere of disorder and fear. The gale is 'muttering' (l. 2), the waves are 'careering' (l. 5), for example. This effect is heightened by using **military imagery**: the 'death-wind' is 'breasting' (l. 7) and 'advancing' (l. 8) as if it were going into battle. There is a real sense of danger.

**Pause for thought**

Why do you think Whitman never allows us to be sure about whether there was a wreck? Do you think the poem is more effective *because* we are not sure?

The poet refers to the 'Waves, air, midnight' as a 'trinity' (ll. 4 and 14), which is perhaps an ironic link to the Christian trinity of God the Father, Son and Holy Ghost. The violent trinity in the poem seems closer to the devil than to God — especially with the reference to 'demoniac laughter' (l. 3). Perhaps the poet is questioning who has power over the elements: God, or a more evil force.

There is a lot of **alliteration** in the poem to link ideas together and create sound effects, such as in line 6 where the repeated 's' sounds reflect the hissing sounds of the snow storm.

## Ideas to consider

* Does the narrator really see a 'wreck' and 'red signal' (l. 9) out at sea, or is it an optical illusion caused by the storm?
* If so, is the wreck the cause of the 'dim, weird forms' (l. 13) that appear to struggle in the water? If not, what could those forms be?

# 'Sonnet 130'

## What happens?

This is one of over 150 sonnets written by Shakespeare. Through it he both mocks other writers of sonnets who use clichés in their writing and praises his own lover.

He looks at the techniques of other poets, who praise their lovers by making romantic but wildly exaggerated comparisons (such as comparing lips with coral or voices with music), and vows to tell the truth about his own lover. The final

couplet shows that although he has been honest in describing her, he still knows her to be 'rare' and special — perhaps more so than other women who have 'false' comparisons made about them.

## Structure

The sonnet is tightly structured. It has a **precise rhyme scheme** of ABAB CDCD EFEF GG, a pattern so often used by Shakespeare that it has become known as a 'Shakespearean sonnet'. It is made up of **iambic pentameters**, so has a gentle rhythm.

## Language and imagery

The poem is written in the **first person**, but that does not necessarily mean that Shakespeare was in love: he wrote for his patron, the Earl of Southampton.

The first line **surprises** us. In a typical love poem, we may expect a lover's eyes to 'shine brighter than the sun', but Shakespeare deliberately turns this stereo-typical **simile** on its head: he claims his lover's eyes are 'nothing like the sun'.

The poem continues, systematically, to consider other similes often used by lovers — and to reject them. In total eight comparisons are explored. The poet is expressing his own true love by rejecting false clichés.

The similes develop as the poem goes on. Lines 1–4 each focus on one of the woman's features (her eyes, lips, breasts and hair). However, warming to his theme, Shakespeare expands his argument by using two lines per feature in lines 5–12 (her cheeks, breath, voice and movement).

 **Pause for thought**

> Do you think that Shakespeare was a more genuine lover than the poets who praised their mistresses with wildly exaggerated images?

The final **rhyming couplet** contains the main message of the poem. His exclamation, 'by heaven' (l. 13), is used to emphasise his point as some people might say 'God!' today, but it could also suggest he is thankful for his 'rare' love. He believes her to be more special to him than any woman 'belied with false compare', or mocked by untrue comparisons.

## Ideas to consider

* The poem is focused solely on the woman's appearance. Does this suggest that Shakespeare thought that looks were everything, or does his description of her hint at what she was like as a person too?

# 'My Last Duchess'

## What happens?

The Duke is showing a guest a picture of his former wife, the last Duchess, painted by a famous artist. It is a private picture, hidden behind a curtain. The Duke tells the listener about his former wife — how she was easily flattered and loved attention. He resents the fact that she did not value his 'gift of a nine-hundred-years-old name' (l. 33) any more

> ### Glossary
> **mantle** *(l. 16)* loose, sleeveless cloak
> **munificence** *(l. 49)* generosity
> **dowry** *(l. 51)* money paid to a bridegroom by a bride's father

than little day-to-day pleasures she enjoyed, and he was too proud to 'stoop' (l. 43) to tell her off. Finally he 'gave commands' (l. 45) and — we assume — had her murdered. It is only at the end of the poem that we realise the person he is talking to is the envoy from a Count, the father of the Duke's bride-to-be. The Duke claims not to be interested in his new wife's dowry, but perhaps we wonder.

## Structure

The poem consists of pairs of **rhyming couplets** (or **heroic couplets**). The rhymes are disguised because most lines use **enjambement**, so the poem sounds more like natural speech. It is written in **iambic pentameters**, which also contribute to the natural style.

## Language and imagery

The poem is a **dramatic monologue**. We take on the role of the listener along with the Count's envoy, and as we do so we gradually work out the narrative. The words seem very convincing, helped particularly by the Duke's pauses and hesitations (e.g. l. 22, ll. 31–32).

Although only one character speaks, we learn much about the Duke and the Duchess, and something about the artist Frà Pandolf and the Count's envoy. We are not told everything directly: we **infer** details, or read between the lines. For example, we are not told for certain what relationship the Duchess had with the artist or how the Duchess behaved in front of her husband. We know the Duke is a man used to being obeyed, and he tells us: 'I gave commands;/Then all smiles stopped together' (ll. 45–46). This is a **euphemism**, enabling the Duke to avoid stating outright that the Duchess died, which is typical of the **ambiguity** present in the poem.

**Pause for thought**

> Is the statue as valuable to the Duke as the painting of his last wife? If so, will the Duke value his new wife in the same heartless way?

**Key point**

Ferrara is in what is now northern Italy. It used to be an independent state, governed by a rich and powerful duke. In this poem, Browning takes on the persona of an imagined Duke of Ferrara.

The Duke appears to be **critical**: 'She had/A heart — how shall I say? — too soon made glad' (ll. 21–22). He also seems **proud** (he highlights his family name, and would not 'stoop'), **heartless** (he shows no regret for his wife's death), **confident** (he tells the story to the envoy, apparently without fearing that it could jeopardise his next marriage), and **cold** (he seems to appreciate works of art more than people).

## Ideas to consider

* It is significant that the poem ends as it began, with the Duke showing the envoy a piece from his art collection. Yet while the first piece was a portrait of his dead wife, the second is a bronze statue of Neptune 'Taming a sea-horse' (l. 55). Perhaps this suggests that the Duke likes to tame people too?
* Do you have any sympathy with the Duke? And the Duchess?
* With what message will the envoy return to the Count?

# 'The Laboratory'

## What happens?

It is not immediately clear who is speaking in this **dramatic monologue** — but clues gradually suggest that it is a rich woman, a courtier who often dances 'at the King's' (l. 12). She seems so jealous of her rival that she is prepared to kill her, which is why the monologue takes place in an alchemist's. She is watching him as he creates a poison that she will use to murder the woman who has 'ensnared' (l. 30) the man she herself loves. She is so delighted with the result that she is prepared to pay the alchemist with all her jewels and gold.

## Structure

The poem consists of twelve stanzas (each numbered, a little like chapters in a novel). Each stanza is made up of two **rhyming couplets** (so the rhyme scheme is AABB), perhaps because the poet wanted to suggest the story is ancient or historic.

### Glossary

**Ancien Régime** French for 'old rule'; specifically, the system of government in France before the Revolution of 1789.
**prithee** *(l. 4)* please
**brave** (l. 14) mighty, splendid, admirable
**phial** *(l. 15)* a small glass bottle, usually used for medicine
**filigree** *(l. 20)* delicate metalwork (often in a precious metal)
**minion** *(l. 29)* a favourite child, servant or girl

## Language and imagery

Because the poem is a monologue, it is written in the **present tense** and so contains drama and tension. We are drawn into the narrative and wonder what will happen.

It contains **archaic phrases** (such as 'prithee' and 'minion') to anchor the story in the past, as if it is a fairy tale. Yet there is a tension between the historical feel of the poem and the immediacy of the story that unfolds.

The speaker reveals a lot about herself. For instance, she is not meek, as her lover and rival assume her to be when they imagine she is in the 'drear/Empty church' (ll. 7–8), but **vengeful** and **bitter**. She is **curious** — she wants to know about the ingredients of the poisons (stanza 4). She is also **cautious**: she wears a mask throughout and ensures that the alchemist brushes the dust off before she grants him a final kiss (stanza 12).

**Alliteration** is used in places to emphasise and link ideas, such as 'Pound at thy powder' (l. 10) and 'Brand, burn up, bite into its grace' (l. 39). The harsh 'p' and 'b' sounds help stress the woman's anger, as if she is spitting out the words.

## Ideas to consider

* Not everything is solved for us. For example, we know very little about the woman's lover and why she is prepared to go to such lengths to keep him for herself. And why are *two* women (Pauline and Elise) mentioned in stanza 6, when the woman seems to concentrate on *one* rival throughout the rest of the poem?

* The subtitle to the poem is 'Ancien Régime', as if the writer wants to suggest that the subject of the poem is in the past. Yet many of the themes are relevant today — including jealousy, vengefulness, and the lengths people (like the alchemist) will go to for money.

**Key point**

The French court was seen as particularly decadent, which is one factor that led to the Revolution. Browning reflects this decadence in the poem.

# 'Ulysses'

## What happens?

1 Tennyson sets his poem many years after Ulysses' previous adventures, when Ulysses and his wife have become 'aged' (l. 3). He feels 'idle' (l. 1) and resentful of his people, whom he calls a 'savage race' (l. 4) and who do not respect him ('know not me': l. 5).

2 For these reasons he decides to travel again, to get the most out of the rest of his life. He is proud of his fame ('I am become a name': l. 11). He wishes

to maximise the time that remains to him ('everyhour...saved/From...eternal silence': ll. 26–27), to make new discoveries and 'follow knowledge' (l. 31).

3 He arranges to hand over rule of Ithaca to his 'Well-loved' (l. 35) son, Telemachus, whom he sees as more suited to the task than he is.

4 Finally he prepares his ship with his faithful mariners. They are all aware that this is likely to be their final voyage and that they will never return, but Ulysses hopes 'Some work of noble note, may yet be done' (l. 52). He encourages his men, reminding them that although they are old and weak, they are 'strong in will' (l. 69) and will not give up.

## Structure

The poem consists of four sections (like paragraphs), each dealing with a different part of Ulysses' preparations to set sail again. Throughout, Tennyson uses **iambic pentameters**. These sound like natural speech, although sometimes Tennyson uses the iambic rhythm to great effect. The final line has a stress on all the key words and is a strong rallying cry to the mariners: 'To <u>strive</u>, to <u>seek</u>, to <u>find</u>, and <u>not</u> to <u>yield</u>'.

## Language and imagery

The poem is a **dramatic monologue**. The language is fitting for a great leader. Ulysses uses balanced sentences, such as 'I cannot rest from travel: I will drink/Life to the lees' (ll. 6–7) and 'He works his work, I mine' (l .43), which are memorable.

We learn much about Ulysses. He is **old**, with a 'gray spirit' (l. 30); but his statement, 'I am a part of all that I have met' (l. 18), shows his awareness that **all experiences shape us** in some way. He is **realistic**, aware that Telemachus will rule Ithaca better than he has done through 'slow prudence' (l. 36). Yet he is also **impatient** to be off, and looks to the future. He has strong bonds to his loyal sailors.

He often uses imagery. For example, there is a **metaphor** of himself as a metal tool or armour gaining 'rust' when he wishes to 'shine in use' (l. 23).

### Key point

Another name for Ulysses is Odysseus. He was a hero during the Trojan Wars (smuggling soldiers into Troy inside the 'gift' of a wooden horse was his idea). He then experienced many adventures in the course of his return home to Ithaca. On his arrival he found his wife beset by many suitors who all believed him to be dead.

## Ideas to consider

- The poem encourages people not to give up and to make the most of their lives.
- Do you admire Ulysses for his enthusiasm and strength of purpose, or criticise him for leaving his country and its problems to Telemachus? (And what about his wife?)
- The poem was written after the death of Tennyson's close friend, Arthur Hallam. Perhaps writing the poem helped give Tennyson the will to pick up his life again and carry on.

# 'The Village Schoolmaster'

## What happens?

The poem describes a schoolmaster in a small rural school. It describes his attitude to his pupils — and theirs to him — and then outlines his accomplishments. He was skilled in practical subjects like writing and sums and measuring land. He could debate with the parson and use long, impressive words, all of which amazed the villagers.

### Glossary

**furze** *(l. 2)* gorse, a heathland shrub with yellow flowers

**gay** *(l. 2)* cheerful

**boding** *(l. 7)* expectant, waiting

**cipher** *(l. 16)* do arithmetic

**presage** *(l. 17)* predict

**gauge** *(l. 18)* estimate the area of a piece of land

## Structure

The poem is written in **rhyming couplets**. Most are **end-stopped** so the rhymes are obvious, and they contribute to the light, upbeat tone of the poem. The lines are **iambic pentameters** and so sound like natural speech.

## Language and imagery

The poem is written in the **first person**, but we have no idea who the speaker is. We only know that he knew the village and its inhabitants well.

The schoolmaster was good at his job. The poet states he was 'skilled to rule' (l. 3), 'kind' (l. 13) and had a great 'love…[of] learning' (l. 14). This suggests he was an ideal teacher.

However, we also learn that the schoolmaster could be 'severe…and stern' (l. 5); and

### Key point

The poem in the *Anthology* is an extract from a much longer poem, *The Deserted Village*, based on a village in Ireland. In it Goldsmith describes a village deserted due to financial hardship and looks back to an idealised past.

(arguably a greater criticism) when debating with the parson he used 'words of learned length and thundering sound' (l. 21) just for the sake of impressing his audience. He was obviously concerned with keeping up his educated appearance.

## Pause for thought

**The poet seems both to admire the schoolmaster and to mock him. Which idea do you think comes across more strongly?**

We also learn a lot about the villagers. The fact that the small rural school-house is called a 'mansion' (l. 3) is ironic, but it also suggests that the villagers lived in tiny dwellings. They had little education, being easily impressed by the schoolmaster's learning: 'The village all declared how much he knew' (l. 15). It seems even to have been the subject of local gossip — 'the story ran that he could gauge' (l. 18). They seem to have been proud of their schoolmaster.

## Ideas to consider

* Goldsmith uses irony to great effect. Having said that the villagers admired all the schoolmaster knew, he undercuts this by saying, ''Twas certain he could write, and cipher too' (l. 16) — rather basic skills.
* Goldsmith presents us with a community in which the parson and the schoolmaster are superior to everyone else: social divisions are fixed. However, perhaps the financial crisis that caused the village to be deserted was partly a result of the rigid class structure.

# 'The Eagle'

## What happens?

In this brief poem (Tennyson subtitled it 'A Fragment') we see the world from an eagle's eye view. The powerful bird is poised on the edge of a high cliff, watching for prey; when he sees it he swoops down to the sea like a thunderbolt to claim it.

David Macias/SPL

## Structure

The poem consists of two **triplets** (or stanzas of three lines rhyming together). We can perhaps see the tight, pared-down structure as conveying something of the gaunt, forceful bird.

## Language and imagery

The poem is written in the **present tense**, which adds tension and drama.

The eagle is **personified**. He has 'hands' (l. 1), and as he 'stands' (l. 3) on his crag, he 'watches' (l. 5) intently. He reminds us of a king or army general surveying the scene. There is a sense that he is the master.

The use of **pronouns** in the poem is interesting. The eagle is given ownership over '<u>his</u> mountain walls' (l. 5); and the sea 'beneath <u>him</u> crawls' (l. 4) almost as if it were subservient to him. This increases the sense of majesty and power.

The **imagery** in the poem is striking. The eagle is placed in the centre of things, 'Ring'd with the azure world' (l. 3), as if everything revolves around him. The sea is 'wrinkled' (l. 4) below him, a vivid adjective to describe the far-away waves. The final **simile** is also forceful: the eagle falls 'like a thunderbolt' (l. 6). This gives him huge power and hints at the destruction of his prey.

There is **alliteration** in the poem: 'He <u>c</u>lasps the <u>c</u>rag with <u>c</u>rookèd hands' and '<u>l</u>onely <u>l</u>ands' (ll. 1–2). This  links ideas and further 'tightens' the poem.

## Ideas to consider

- It is interesting that although Tennyson gave the eagle characteristics of a powerful man, mankind is not mentioned in the poem. (Are the 'lonely lands' (l. 2) places without humans or without any life at all?) Perhaps there is a message here: Tennyson may be hinting that humans are not as all-powerful as they would like to believe.
- We are given the eagle's point of view. He considers himself strong, mighty and in control: he has power over life and death.

# 'Inversnaid'

## What happens?

Hopkins describes a favourite scene in the Highlands. He follows the path of a burn as it falls over a small waterfall and down a mountain to a lake, then focuses in (like a cinematic shot) on some froth being spun round on the fast-moving water. In the third stanza he describes the burn's banks and surroundings. The final stanza is a passionate plea to people to conserve such areas 'Of wet and of wildness' (l. 14) — a message that is even more important today than when Hopkins wrote 'Inversnaid'.

## Structure

The poem consists of four equal stanzas of four lines. Each stanza is made up of two **rhyming couplets**, rhyming AABB. This scheme creates a bouncing pace,

reminiscent of the quick-flowing water. The lines are on average eight syllables long; the variation perhaps suggests the random path of the water.

## Language and imagery

The poem is in the **present tense**. Hopkins describes the scene in such detail that he seems to be personally pointing different features out to us — especially as the first word is 'This'. We are drawn into the poem.

Hopkins typically uses language in an original and imaginative way. He invents **compound words** by joining together two words that are not usually associated with each other, like 'rollrock' (l. 2) and 'windpuff' (l. 5). He also creates **portmanteau words** like 'twindles' (l. 6), which seems to be a mixture of 'twists', 'twitches' and 'dwindles'. These are all words which would make very little sense outside the poem but seem perfect for what Hopkins is describing.

### Glossary

**Inversnaid** a place in the Highlands of Scotland, overlooking Loch Lomond
**burn** (l. 1) small stream
**flutes** (l. 4) frills, becomes frilly
**degged** (l. 9) sprinkled (a northern dialect word)
**braes** (l. 10) steep banks, hillsides
**flitches** (l. 11) usually cuts from a tree; here, ragged tufts
**ash** (l. 12) a rowan tree, which has orange-red berries
**bereft** (l. 13) robbed, deprived, bereaved

There is a sort of **extended metaphor** in the first stanza: the burn is likened to a horse, not only because of its 'horseback brown' colour (l. 1) — from the peat the water passes through on the moors — but because it seems to be 'roaring down' a 'highroad' (l. 2), 'home' (l. 4) to the lake, its 'fleece' (l. 3) (or mane) flying.

The language of the second stanza is more complex. Hopkins describes a little ball of fawn-coloured froth on the surface of the water being tossed over a dark whirlpool. (The pool is dark because it is in the shadow of the fells.) The pool could be an image of 'Despair' (like Hell), or maybe it is so dark that Despair itself could be drowning in it.

Hopkins uses frequent **alliteration** and **consonance** in the poem to great effect. For example, the 'r' sounds in 'rollrock highroad roaring down' (l. 2) suggest the rushing pace of the stream, while there are heavy 'd' sounds in 'rounds and rounds Despair to drowning' (l. 8). Note the echoing **assonance** too, such as 'rollrock highroad roaring down', which further intensify the sound effects in the poem.

### Pause for thought

> To whom might Hopkins have wanted to deliver his message?

The tone changes in the final stanza. Hopkins uses the word 'bereft' (l. 13) to suggest that the loss of such environments would be like the death of a loved one for us. He poses a **rhetorical question** to make us think about the importance of natural environments.

## Ideas to consider

* It is interesting that the light puff of froth *escapes* the whirlpool in stanza 2. Perhaps Hopkins, a fervent Christian, is suggesting that Despair is not inevitable — that if one is 'light' enough through faith in God, one will 'float' over troubles.
* The final plea for the conservation of wild places contains **rhetorical devices** like **repetition** and **alliteration** and the use of a **passive verb**, 'Let them be left' (l. 14), almost like a politician's speech.

# 'Sonnet'

## What happens?

The poem is a simple expression of the poet's fondness for summer. He describes the clouds, the flowers, the birds and the insects.

## Structure

The poem is, of course, a sonnet, consisting of seven **rhyming couplets**. Sonnets are a traditional form for love poetry. Here Clare is expressing his love not for a woman, but for a season and a landscape.

There is no punctuation at all in the poem, which emphasises its simplicity.

### Glossary

**Mare blobs** *(l. 4)* marsh marigolds

**drain** *(l. 4)* gully at the bottom of the meadow for excess water

**flag** *(l. 8)* wild iris

## Language and imagery

In a sense the poet is **like a film director**. He begins with a wide-angle lens and describes the clouds, then a distant view of the marsh marigolds. They are so distant that he doesn't see them individually, but as a golden stain on the 'meadow drain' (l. 4). He then zooms in on details such as the Moor Hen, and finally he gives us a close-up of the insects. The effect is to give us a whole panorama of the scene and encourage us to appreciate every detail.

The language used is very **simple**, almost childlike. There is **repetition** of 'I love' and adjectives such as 'clear', and most of the words are of one syllable. It is as if the poet did not want to tarnish his vision with anything more complex.

The poem **appeals to our senses**. For example, we *see* the white and gold flowers, *hear* the 'rustle' (l. 6) of the reeds, *feel* the 'winds' (l. 12) and *smell* the 'hay grass' (l. 11).

The poet uses a **range of imagery**. Summer itself is **personified** as a cheery person 'beaming forth' (l. 1), while there is a **mixed metaphor** to describe the clouds: they are both 'white wool sack[s]' and ships in full sail (l. 2).

**Alliteration** is used to link ideas and create sound effects. Here you can hear the wind: 'Where reed clumps rustle like a wind shook wood' (l. 6).

## Ideas to consider

* The poem glorifies the scene that Clare portrays. It is interesting that he highlights the colours white and gold, to suggest a majestic or even religious atmosphere. Do you think that, by extension, Clare is glorifying *all* of nature?

* Clare had been through a personal crisis just before he wrote this poem. How do you think that writing the 'Sonnet' may have helped him?

# Themes

As you read this section, ask yourself:
➢ What are the most important themes in Heaney's poetry?
➢ What are the most important themes in Clarke's poetry?
➢ What themes do they share — and how do they treat these themes?

When we talk about themes in poetry, we mean ideas that recur in a poet's work. They are usually ideas that the poet feels are important and wants to explore in some way. They can be triggered by many things: perhaps a memory, or something the poet has experienced, or the world around them. The poet returns to these ideas and looks at them from different angles in different poems. Often themes are interrelated: Heaney, for example, looks at both childhood and the continuity of a family through each generation.

It is difficult to define the themes of a particular poet precisely. Different people will have different readings of poems, so interpretation has to be taken into account. The general drift of a theme is usually clear, although the specific titles people give to each theme may be different.

## Heaney

### Ireland

Every poem by Heaney featured in the *Anthology* is set in Ireland. Sometimes place names are referred to specifically to anchor the poem, such as 'the clear Bann River' in 'Perch' and 'Toner's bog' in 'Digging'. Heaney places emphasis on the particular features of the Irish landscape, the 'crow-black fields' ('At a Potato Digging') and the 'flax-dam' ('Death of a Naturalist'). Irish farmers' ways and the vocabulary peculiar to their work are also featured: he talks about the 'headrig' of a ploughed field ('Follower') and the 'Wicker creels' that are used for gathering crops ('At a Potato Digging'). He also includes typically Irish words and phrases. These are perhaps most poignant in 'Mid-Term Break', where old men tell the young Heaney they are 'sorry for my trouble' when his younger brother dies; they are also used more light-heartedly, as in 'Perch we called "grunts"' ('Perch').

Because Heaney's poetry is rooted so deeply in his homeland, we gain both an impression of his love for his country and a privileged insider's view — Ireland as the Irish see it.

## His childhood

In many poems Heaney looks back at a happy rural childhood spent on the family farm or in the countryside with friends. 'Perch', 'Blackberry-Picking', 'Death of a Naturalist', 'Digging' and 'Follower' all touch on this. He was content to fish, gather blackberries or frogspawn, or help his father and grandfather on the farm. Yet all was not perfect. Both 'Blackberry-Picking' and 'Death of a Naturalist' end in disappointment when the treasure-store of blackberries rots and the bullfrogs scare the young Heaney — already he was learning hard lessons. Looking back on these days from an adult's perspective, Heaney is able to show us both the child's eye view and a more mature reflection. He uses this to make us think about wider issues, such as what it is to be disillusioned or to be honest with oneself.

'Mid-Term Break' is slightly different to the other childhood poems, as it describes a family tragedy and how Heaney reacts to the sudden loss of his younger brother. Here he is treated as a grown-up: 'old men standing up to shake my hand'; he is aware that his childhood is nearly over.

## His family

Heaney is interested in exploring the idea of links between generations, of family continuity. He mentions his mother only once ('Mid-Term Break'), but as a man, expected to do 'man's work', he comes back again and again to his father and grandfather in their work and debates whether he should have followed in their footsteps. He writes with pride of his father, 'An expert' ('Follower') and 'By God, the old man could handle a spade' ('Digging'); he says his grandfather 'cut more turf in a day/Than any other man' ('Digging'). He wrestles with the idea that he himself, who once wanted to grow up and plough ('Follower'), should be sitting with a pen in his hand. He rationalises to himself that if he 'digs' into his past with it by writing poetry, he is indeed continuing his father's and grandfather's legacy.

## Nature as an ally

Heaney loves the natural world and knows it intimately (so intimately that he can almost put himself into the mind of a fish in 'Perch'). He describes nature in minute detail and very sensuously, as in 'Bubbles gargled delicately, bluebottles/Wove a strong gauze of sound around the smell' ('Death of a Naturalist'). We are able to see, hear and smell the putrid water in the dam and so can imagine it clearly.

From the emphasis on farming in Heaney's poetry, nature appears to be generous to us. Nature provides us with food (fish, blackberries and, most importantly, potatoes), with warmth (from peat, used as a fuel) and with an income (from food, peat and flax). Heaney celebrates nature's gifts with, for example, his light-hearted descriptions of the 'little flood-slubs, runty and ready' ('Perch'), his rich image of the blackberries with flesh 'sweet/Like thickened wine' ('Blackberry-Picking') and the potatoes 'white as cream' ('At a Potato Digging'). He acknowledges our great debt to nature: we depend utterly upon it.

## Nature as an enemy

Heaney is also respectful of nature, knowing it can be malevolent and more powerful than humans. This is shown in a mild way in 'Blackberry-Picking' when a 'rat-grey fungus' spoils the crop. It is shown more seriously when he describes the potato famine: 'Live skulls, blind-eyed, balanced on/wild higgledy skeletons' ('At a Potato Digging'), and when he barricades himself indoors as if under attack in 'Storm on the Island' when the sea is 'exploding' and 'savage'.

Because of his dependence on nature, much of Heaney's imagery is rooted in the natural world. For example, the labourers picking potatoes are seen as a 'swarm' like busy bees fixed upon their task, while the potatoes themselves are 'scattered/like inflated pebbles' ('At a Potato Digging'). It is this combination of subject and imagery that helps to make Heaney's poetry so successful.

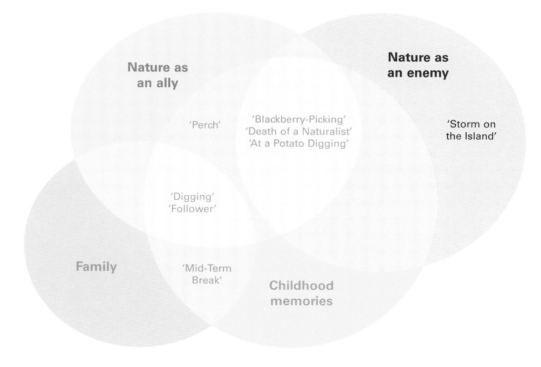

Figure 2 Heaney's themes

# Clarke

It is interesting that there is no single uniting theme in this selection of Clarke's poetry. Although the poems were all written in Wales (and, in the case of 'On the Train', are about her returning from England to Wales), there is not as vivid a sense of that country as there is in Heaney's poems of Ireland. (You might enjoy other poems by Clarke that focus on Welsh mythology and explore Welsh ideas.) Instead, her poems in the *Anthology* give us a range of themes that often overlap and interconnect.

## Her family and motherhood

Clarke explores her feelings towards her family in a number of poems. More specifically, the first three poems in the selection, 'Catrin', 'Baby-sitting' and 'Mali', are about motherhood. We see her becoming a mother, fighting over 'the tight/Red rope of love' when Catrin is born (and she later uses the knowledge gained from having given birth herself to help the ailing ewe in 'A Difficult Birth, Easter 1998': 'I ease my fingers in'). She is then portrayed standing in for an absent mother guarding 'the wrong baby' ('Baby-sitting'), and becoming a grandmother on the unexpectedly early arrival of 'My daughter's daughter' ('Mali'). Her emotions are not necessarily the romantic 'poetic' ones we would expect. As well as expressing love, 'that unmistakable brim and tug of the tide' ('Mali'), she describes a 'struggle' and 'fighting/[Catrin] off'. She is emphatic that her maternal feelings are for her own children only: 'I don't love/This baby' ('Baby-sitting'). She shows the tensions that take place within a family as well as unconditional love. It is interesting that she uses the phrase 'life-sentenced' ('Mali') to express her unending love for her new granddaughter, when we usually associate that phrase with hatred and punishment. Perhaps she is suggesting that such intense inescapable love has a price.

We see Clarke with her own mother in 'Cold Knap Lake', when her mother is the 'heroine' and saves a child from death. This rescue, too, is a type of birth, as though Clarke's mother has brought another girl into the world in addition to the poet herself. Ironically, when the girl is returned to her family, she is 'thrashed for almost drowning': the harsh verb gives us the feeling that it was not the family Clarke would have wanted for her.

The importance of her family to Clarke is also briefly referred to elsewhere. The field-mouse that inspired the poem of that name was brought to her by her 'child', and the contrast between her own happy afternoon with her children and the plight of war-torn Bosnia struck her. In 'A Difficult Birth, Easter 1998', she mentions the 'quiet supper and bottle of wine' she and her husband had been looking forward to, and in 'On the Train' she is anxious to get through to her husband and tell him 'Darling, I'm on the train'.

## Nature

Many of Clarke's poems include references to and descriptions of nature. The birth of Mali is linked to 'late summer heat overspilling into harvest', so the fruitfulness of Clarke's daughter coincides with the wild fruit of nature. There is another great celebration when the ewe that had been thought 'barren' produces twins ('A Difficult Birth, Easter 1998').

Nature is not always beneficent, however. The birth of the twin lambs is difficult. There is a sense that the child almost drowns in 'Cold Knap Lake' because of the 'water's long green silk' or something else, mysterious and 'shadowy', beneath the surface.

Nature provokes and inspires an emotional response in Clarke, but it is also portrayed as reflecting her emotions. The autumn poplars, although beautiful with their trembling 'gold' leaves, have a 'broken branch', symbolising the death of Clarke's friend, and the rain is 'weeping in the air' ('October').

Clarke is also interested in the part we play in shaping nature. Whereas she is able to help the ewe in labour and so contribute to the natural world, she also recognises that we harm it. In 'The Field-Mouse' she writes 'the field lies bleeding', referring both to the harvested hay field with its injured animals and to the fields (which symbolise nature in general) of Bosnia damaged in the conflict.

## Death

Clarke invites us to consider death in various ways. Her personal reaction to the death of her friend is to consider her own unknown 'death-day' and work as hard as she can to beat it ('October'). The death of a single field-mouse makes her think of thousands of dead in a country far away. She expresses through her nightmare how impossible it is for us to understand the horrors fully: 'I dream the children dance in grass/their bones brittle as mouse-ribs, the air/stammering with gunfire' ('The Field-Mouse'). The vivid image of 'the blazing bone-ship' ('On the Train') conveys the impossibility of escaping death for those caught up in a rail disaster. In none of these poems does Clarke try directly to describe the dead people; she illustrates her emotions through her imagery.

The child in 'Cold Knap Lake', of course, escapes death — but only just. The final couplet of the poem, 'All lost things lie under closing water/in that lake with the poor man's daughter', suggests that something *has* died. We, the readers, are left to determine what.

**Key point**

Both Heaney and Clarke write from an intensely personal point of view: each writes about their *own* thoughts, memories, emotions and reactions. They do not write from the point of view of anyone else, which gives a feeling of honesty and depth to their work. Every poem by Heaney and Clarke in the *Anthology* is written in the first person.

## Reactions to outside events

Some of the poems in the selection give the poet's reactions to major events — we would have heard about them on the news and they would have occupied many pages in the newspapers. It is interesting that the two poems with tragic themes ('The Field-Mouse' and 'On the Train') do not refer specifically to the war in Bosnia or the Paddington rail crash (although Clarke writes elsewhere that these are the sources). This means that the poems could be about any war or any train disaster, and gives them a more universal feeling. However, the one story of good news, the Good Friday peace deal, is described in detail: 'the Irish peace deal close', 'they slog it out in Belfast' ('A Difficult Birth, Easter 1998'). The politicians' achievement is compared to the miracle of an elderly ewe giving birth.

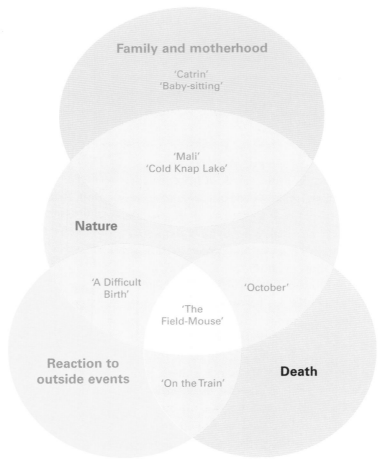

Figure 3 Clarke's themes

# Themes shared by Heaney and Clarke

Heaney and Clarke explore some similar ideas through their poetry.

## Nature

Both poets are interested in writing about nature, from tiny details to broad landscapes. Heaney gives us a close-up view of a blackberry, 'a glossy purple clot' ('Blackberry-Picking'), and of the 'jellied/Specks' of frogspawn ('Death of a Naturalist'), while Clarke notices the 'black eyes' of a dying creature, 'two sparks burning' ('The Field-Mouse'). At the other extreme, Heaney gives us a wide-angle view of a field 'from hedge to headland' ('At a Potato Digging') and of the sea ('Storm on the Island'), and Clarke shows us 'the fields, the grass, the racing leaves' ('October').

Heaney's work is in general more connected to the soil — 'gravelly ground', 'soggy peat' ('Digging') and 'crumbled earth' ('At a Potato Digging') — because it is centred on nature itself. Clarke, on the other hand, uses her own experience of working alongside nature — haymaking in 'The Field-Mouse', the birth of the lambs in 'A Difficult Birth, Easter 1998' — as a way in to investigating wider issues.

## The family

Another thematic interest that the poets share is family and how generations of a family interrelate. Heaney concentrates on the male side ('Digging', 'Follower') while Clarke explores the female side ('Catrin', 'Baby-sitting', 'Mali'). For Heaney, continuity from generation to generation is important. He describes skills passed down from father to son: 'the old man could handle a spade./Just like his old man' ('Digging'), and he asks himself whether he should not be out there digging too. Clarke is more aware of differences between parents and their children, highlighting the 'love and conflict' that she shares with her daughter ('Catrin'). Yet she also acknowledges the tie that unites three generations when her granddaughter is born: 'My daughter's daughter…/Even the sea could not draw me from her' ('Mali').

## Death

Although it is not a major theme in this selection of his work, Heaney does explore death in his poetry. The immediate aftermath of the tragic death of his young brother is movingly described — Heaney can only begin to understand his feelings when he is alone with the body in its small coffin. The simple final line, 'A four-foot box, a foot for every year', is beautiful in its matter-of-factness ('Mid-Term Break'). Clarke writes poignantly of the death of her friend in 'October'. The coffin is 'lighter/than hare-bones on men's shoulders' and the wind and rain seem to echo the sombre mood.

Clarke goes on to write about deaths in the wider world of people she does not know, in 'On the Train' and 'The Field-Mouse'. In each case she imagines the consequences of those deaths (she paints a surreal nightmare scenario in 'On the Train', where 'in the rubble of suburban kitchens/the wolves howl into silent telephones'). She also thinks about her own instincts to protect her children and her family. Heaney examines the deaths of the 'Millions' who 'rotted' as a result of the famine in Ireland in the nineteenth century ('At a Potato Digging'). He uses the repugnant image 'you still smell the running sore' to show that this intense horror has not been forgotten.

Heaney also uses the idea of death metaphorically in 'Death of a Naturalist' when he describes the death of his innocence. As a child, he was terrified by 'angry' 'gross-bellied frogs' and saw their presence as 'vengeance' for having taken frogspawn from the flax-dam. Perhaps his sense of guilt manifested itself. The use of the word 'Death' in the title suggests that something was lost to him for ever as a result of the experience.

## Conflict

At times both poets focus on conflict. You could argue that Heaney grapples with memories of childhood's internal conflict in 'Death of a Naturalist': the frogs are certainly warlike, 'Poised like mud grenades'. In a very different way he uses the imagery of warfare in 'Storm on the Island': 'Space is a salvo./We are bombarded'. The power of the wind and waves is likened to a military machine, which emphasises its might and destructiveness.

Clarke looks both at personal conflicts such as the 'Fierce confrontation[s]' she has with her daughter ('Catrin'), and at wider conflicts such as the Irish problems ('A Difficult Birth, Easter 1998') and the war in Bosnia ('The Field-Mouse'). In 'The Field-Mouse' she describes how 'The air hums with jets' and how the radio broadcasts 'terrible news'; her nightmare includes 'air/stammering with gunfire'. The main way in which she shows the conflict, however, is through metaphor: the dead mouse and the 'bleeding' hay field in Wales represent the death and destruction taking place on a far greater scale hundreds of miles away.

### Review your learning

Quick questions (answers are given on page 102):

1 What are the main themes in Heaney's poetry?

2 What are the main themes in Clarke's poetry?

3 Which of the following themes does Heaney *not* write about?

   war        childhood       death        nature        his family

4 Which of the following themes does Clarke *not* write about?

   war        death        her family        the future        nature

Longer questions:

5 Complete Table 1 to record some poems on various themes that you might want to compare. Write down any poems which are appropriate: you will find that there are a number of poems that could fill each box.

Table 1 Themes in Heaney and Clarke

| | Clarke | Heaney |
|---|---|---|
| Nature | | |
| The family | | |
| Death | | |
| Conflict | | |

6 Briefly sum up each poet's attitude to the four themes they share.

# Style

As you read this section, ask yourself:
- ➤ Why is it important to recognise a poem's viewpoint?
- ➤ What do the setting and atmosphere contribute to a poem?
- ➤ How do symbolism and imagery affect a poem?
- ➤ How have the poets used rhythm, rhyme and metre?

As well as considering *what* a poet writes about, it is important to consider *how* they write. In good poetry, the way in which ideas are expressed helps to convey the message or to emphasise what is being said. This chapter looks at the styles adopted by Heaney and Clarke and a number of the poets in the Pre-1914 Poetry Bank, pointing out key aspects. Of course, it is often hard to look at each aspect in isolation because the language is so dense that techniques overlap each other, but it is important to recognise the main ones.

If you are not familiar with some of the literary terms used in this chapter, you can look them up in the 'Glossary of literary terms' at the end of the book. Table 2 on pages 82–83 summarises the poetic techniques used in all the poems discussed in this guide.

## Viewpoint

All the poems by Heaney and Clarke in your *Anthology* are written in the **first person**. Their poems are intensely personal and convey the poets' own thoughts and feelings. There is a sense that the poets are baring their souls and we are privileged to read about things that are so intimate and obviously important to them. For example:
- Heaney grapples with his conscience over whether he is letting down his father and grandfather by not becoming a farmer: 'I've no spade to follow men like them' ('Digging'). We also see his guilty frustration with his elderly father who 'keeps stumbling/Behind me, and will not go away' ('Follower').
- Clarke writes intimately about motherhood. She is disarmingly honest about the 'love and conflict' that she shares with her daughter in 'Catrin' and the lack of emotion she has for a baby not her own: 'her nose/Will stream disgustingly and the perfume/Of her breath will fail to enchant me' ('Baby-sitting').

Some of the pre-1914 poems also use the **first person** and, again, we are witness to the poets' innermost thoughts. For example:

* Jonson writes movingly about his emotions in 'On my first Sonne' and we see the tension he feels between mourning his beloved child, his 'best piece of poetrie', and convincing himself that the boy is in a better place with God.
* Tichborne in his 'Elegy' mourns his own imminent death in a surprisingly calm, controlled, lucid manner: 'My glass is full, and now my glass is run;/And now I live, and now my life is done.'
* Clare writes frankly about the joy a beautiful landscape can give. His 'Sonnet' is an outpouring of gratitude for a sunny summer's day.

However, a number of other poems written in the first person do not tell us the poets' own thoughts but convey those of fictional characters. The poets have each adopted a **persona**, presenting us with what they imagine to be the character's thoughts. The style in which they write reflects the character they are presenting. For instance:

* Wordsworth takes on the persona of a woman who is wild with worry because she has lost contact with her only son, in 'The Affliction of Margaret'. The long, detailed poem suggests the length of time she has spent grieving and wondering over his absence.
* In 'The Laboratory' by Browning (another example of a male poet adopting a female persona) we see a woman bent on vengeance, fascinated by the method the alchemist in her pay is using to murder her rival.
* Hardy becomes a jobbing soldier in 'The Man He Killed' and we see a simple man grappling to make sense of war. He uses dialect and slang appropriate to the character.

Two poems in the selection, Blake's 'The Little Boy Lost/Found' and Tennyson's 'The Eagle', are written in the **third person**, from the perspective of an omniscient (all-knowing) narrator. The poets act as reporters or storytellers, relaying to us what happens. At the same time, of course, what they tell us is carefully chosen to contribute to the subject, atmosphere and tone of what they are writing about.

# Setting and atmosphere

Heaney and Clarke both convey the setting of their poems in vivid terms. This is not merely to set the scene for us, but to create atmosphere too. For example:

* Heaney sets 'Blackberry-Picking' in 'Late August, [with] heavy rain and sun', which builds up a picture of a cloying day, appropriate to the rich yet excessive harvest he goes on to describe. Details such as 'green and heavy headed/Flax had rotted there' in 'Death of a Naturalist' suggest a nightmarish landscape, perfect for the horrors that are to come in the poem.

- Clarke immediately sets warning bells ringing in the reader's head when she sets 'The Field-Mouse' in 'Summer, and the long grass is a snare drum'. Not only does the metaphor suggest the sounds of insects in the grass, but the word 'snare' reminds us of traps and death.

Creating a setting which produces atmosphere was also important for the pre-1914 poets:

- Whitman begins 'Patrolling Barnegat' with 'Wild, wild the storm', the repetition suggesting the strength of the weather.
- Tennyson actually seems to be pointing out the backdrop for us: 'There lies the port; the vessel puffs her sail:/There gloom the dark broad seas ('Ulysses').' The use of 'gloom' hints that the enthusiastic sailors will have challenges to face, and so creates tension in the poem.

## Symbolism

Symbols are used by poets rather like pictures in a book — to illustrate a point more clearly, or to leave a vivid impression of an idea. A **symbol** is one thing that represents another thing or idea. It can be the central theme of a poem, or can develop a particular idea within a poem. Heaney, Clarke and the pre-1914 poets sometimes use symbols to enrich or clarify their work. For example:

- The snowdrops by the bedside of Heaney's dead brother are pure and delicate, and symbolise both the pure, sinless nature of the child and his fragility ('Mid-Term Break').
- The innocent and vulnerable field-mouse, killed by the harvester in Clarke's poem of the same name, is a symbol of all the innocent and vulnerable people who are killed just as easily in war. The broken branch in 'October' is a symbol of her friend's death.
- The child in Blake's 'The Little Boy Lost/Found' is a symbol for all human beings. Blake is suggesting that we can all wander away into danger and we all need God to bring us back to safety.
- The burn that Hopkins describes in 'Inversnaid' is a symbol of all the water in the world. By showing how the stream is important to the Highland landscape, Hopkins is able to put over his wider point about preserving the 'wet and…wildness'.

## Imagery

Imagery, like symbolism, is a way for poets to add word pictures to their poems. Imagery includes figures of speech such as **similes**, **metaphors** and **personification** to illustrate ideas. These are often most successful when they are tied in with the poet's **themes** (look back at the 'Themes' chapter for more ideas).

Heaney's startling use of metaphor in 'At a Potato Digging' is a good illustration. He describes freshly harvested potatoes as 'live skulls, blind-eyed', a phrase which suggests their knobbly, skull-like shape and indicates that they have not yet sprouted. He repeats the phrase 'live skulls, blind-eyed', but this time it refers to starving people. We see them as little more than skulls, with shrunken skull-like faces and sunken eyes — ironically, their heads appear appallingly like the potatoes which their bodies crave. Most of Heaney's imagery is linked to the themes of his poems in this way, although there are exceptions. 'Follower', for example, uses nautical imagery which likens his father's expertise with the plough to a sailor's expertise with his ship.

Clarke also uses powerful imagery connected to the themes of her poems. In 'Catrin' the recurring metaphor of the umbilical cord as a 'rope' shows mother and daughter still bound together long after the birth. In 'Cold Knap Lake' she refers to the rescued girl being 'dressed in water's long green silk', an eerily beautiful metaphor which makes the water and waterweed seem less threatening than they actually are.

'Tichborne's Elegy' consists almost entirely of metaphors, as it illustrates how life is being cut short: 'My prime of youth is but a frost of cares,/My feast of joy is but a dish of pain'. Here imagery emphasises tragedy. Shakespeare plays with similes in a near-comic way throughout 'Sonnet 130', pretending to try to find images that describe his lover honestly and without using clichés: 'My mistress' eyes are nothing like the sun'.

## Alliteration and assonance

Where imagery could be said to add pictures to a poem, **alliteration** and **assonance** add the sound effects. Sometimes these techniques bind ideas together. Examples are Heaney describing tadpoles as 'jampotfuls of the jellied/Specks' in 'Death of a Naturalist', and Clarke describing how the crowd around the rescued child were 'drawn by the dread of it' ('Cold Knap Lake').

Alliteration works most effectively when the sound of the words echoes the sense. The 'heavy headed/Flax' is made to sound more weighty by the repeated accented 'h', and the frogs appear all the more frightening for their 'coarse croaking', with the emphasis falling on the clicking 'c' sound ('Death of a Naturalist').

Of the pre-1914 poets, Whitman and Hopkins perhaps use these sound effects most effectively. The intensity of the 's' sounds in 'On beachy slush and sand spirts of snow fierce slanting' (where alliteration combines with **consonance**) enables us to hear the snow shooting down the beach, and Whitman describes the 'hoarse roar' of the waves ('Patrolling Barnegat'). Hopkins combines alliteration and assonance in one rushing line, 'His rollrock highroad roaring down', to give an impression of the turbulent, dancing water ('Inversnaid').

Table 2 Poetic techniques

| | First person | Persona | Third person | Iambic pentameter | Regular stanzas | Rhyme |
|---|---|---|---|---|---|---|
| **Heaney** | | | | | | |
| 'Storm on the Island' | ✓ | | | ✓ | | |
| 'Perch' | ✓ | | | | ✓ | ✓ |
| 'Blackberry-Picking' | ✓ | | | ✓ | | |
| 'Death of a Naturalist' | ✓ | | | ✓ | | |
| 'Digging' | ✓ | | | ✓ | | |
| 'Mid-Term Break' | ✓ | | | ✓ | ✓ | |
| 'Follower' | ✓ | | | | ✓ | ✓ |
| 'At a Potato Digging' | ✓ | | | | ✓ | ✓ |
| **Clarke** | | | | | | |
| 'Catrin' | ✓ | | | | | |
| 'Baby-sitting' | ✓ | | | | ✓ | |
| 'Mali' | ✓ | | | | ✓ | |
| 'A Difficult Birth, Easter 1998' | ✓ | | | | ✓ | |
| 'The Field-Mouse' | ✓ | | | | ✓ | |
| 'October' | ✓ | | | ✓ | ✓ | |
| 'On the Train' | ✓ | | | | ✓ | |
| 'Cold Knap Lake' | ✓ | | | | ✓ | |

| | First person | Persona | Third person | Iambic pentameter | Regular stanzas | Rhyme |
|---|---|---|---|---|---|---|
| **Pre-1914 Poetry Bank** | | | | | | |
| 'On my first Sonne' | ✓ | | | | | ✓ |
| 'The Song of the Old Mother' | | ✓ | | | | ✓ |
| 'The Affliction of Margaret' | | ✓ | | | ✓ | ✓ |
| 'The Little Boy Lost/ Found' | | | ✓ | | ✓ | ✓ |
| 'Tichborne's Elegy' | ✓ | | | | ✓ | ✓ |
| 'The Man He Killed' | | ✓ | | | ✓ | ✓ |
| 'Patrolling Barnegat' | ✓ | | | | | ✓ |
| 'Sonnet 130' | (✓) | | | | | ✓ |
| 'My Last Duchess' | | ✓ | | ✓ | | ✓ |
| 'The Laboratory' | | ✓ | | | ✓ | ✓ |
| 'Ulysses' | | ✓ | | ✓ | | |
| 'The Village Schoolmaster' | | ✓ | | ✓ | | ✓ |
| 'The Eagle' | | | ✓ | | ✓ | ✓ |
| 'Inversnaid' | ✓ | | | | ✓ | ✓ |
| 'Sonnet' | ✓ | | | ✓ | | ✓ |

# Rhythm, rhyme and metre

Heaney writes many of his poems in **iambic pentameter**. Some are **blank verse** (such as 'Storm on the Island' and 'Blackberry-Picking'); in others the lines are divided into stanzas, either loosely (as in 'Digging') or more formally (as in 'Mid-Term Break', which consists of three-line stanzas). This rhythm suits his poetry because it has the feel of ordinary speech; we sense that Heaney is talking to us or confiding in us. (It is used so naturally that we may not even realise the rhythm is there unless we count the syllables in the lines.) Often Heaney chooses not to end-stop the lines but uses **enjambement** so that the sense flows on between the lines, adding to the conversational style. He sometimes uses **rhyme** to create effects. The rhyming couplets in 'Perch' are almost onomatopoeic — the **half-rhymes** 'river'/'waver', 'ready'/'body' give an impression of the moving water. At other times rhyme echoes the sense of the words: the ABAB pattern in 'Follower' is like the precise pattern in the field made by the father's skilled ploughing.

Heaney's use of rhythm, rhyme and metre is more traditional than Clarke's. Her poetry is freer: she very rarely uses rhyme and her lines often have a varying number of syllables. She does not use a capital letter at the beginning of a line in any poems apart from the first two in the selection, 'Catrin' and 'Baby-sitting' (which are early works), explaining on her website that to do so is 'old-fashioned'. She does write in **regular stanzas**, however, sometimes altering the form slightly for effect. For example, in 'October', which is based on six-line stanzas, the sixth line of the second stanza flows into the first line of the final stanza, and the final stanza has an extra line. Perhaps this echoes the idea that she wants to pack as much as possible into the time that is left to her, thus 'winning ground'. Similarly, 'Cold Knap Lake', which consists of alternating four-line and six-line stanzas, concludes with a rhyming couplet, which adds to the sense of fairy tale and mystery that she is writing about.

Because of the time when they were written, most of the pre-1914 poems have a tight structure. Stanzas, where used, are of equal length and may chart the progression of a narrative, each stanza dealing with an addition to the 'story' (such as 'The Affliction of Margaret', 'The Man He Killed' and 'The Laboratory'). Many of the poems have a fixed **rhyme scheme**. Sometimes the rhyme scheme is disguised, as in 'My Last Duchess', where the use of enjambement means that the rhyming couplets are not immediately obvious (and so the Duke's words appear more natural). In other poems the rhyme scheme is brought to the fore and is used to emphasise the meaning of the poem. For example, 'The Song of the Old Mother' concludes with 'old' rhyming with 'cold', heavy words to reflect the woman's heaviness of heart. The later poems, such as Whitman's 'Patrolling Barnegat', are less formally structured. Here the lines are much longer than usual and all lines end with an identical musical yet menacing '–ing' rhyme.

# The poets' choice of language

It goes almost without saying that poets choose their style of language carefully to fit their subject matter. Heaney uses childish language in 'Perch' (with words like 'grunts') because the fish remind him of his childhood, and they appear not to have changed since his childhood. In contrast he uses simple, formal language when it is appropriate, as in 'Mid-Term Break'. Clarke uses language full of references to the abundance of nature and the harvest — 'overspilling', 'reddening', 'sweet', 'purple' — when she welcomes her granddaughter into the world in 'Mali'. She uses much more subdued language when writing about her friend's death in 'October': 'our faces/stony, rain, weeping in the air'.

In the pre-1914 selection, there is a great contrast between Tennyson's brief, stark, strictly rhyming fragment of 'The Eagle' and the richly detailed, flowing 'Ulysses'. Much of Hardy's poetry is detailed and romantic, yet in 'The Man He Killed' he deliberately uses simple, colloquial language suitable for the ordinary soldier whose persona he adopts: 'We should have sat us down to wet/Right many a nipperkin!'

## Review your learning

Quick questions: true or false? (Answers are given on page 102.)

1 Both Heaney and Clarke write in the third person.
2 A symbol is an object or image which represents another thing or idea.
3 'I will represent <u>a</u>bsolute <u>a</u>bandonment' ('Baby-sitting') is an example of alliteration.
4 'N<u>i</u>cking and sl<u>i</u>cing' ('Digging') is an example of assonance.
5 'Death of a Naturalist' is written in iambic pentameter.

Longer questions:

6 Choose a poem by Heaney that includes rhyme. Write a paragraph explaining what the rhyme contributes.
7 Choose a poem by Clarke that includes some striking enjambement and try to explain its effect. You could concentrate on two or three lines only.

# Comparing poems

As you read this section, ask yourself:
➤ Which aspects should I concentrate on when comparing poems?
➤ What type of things should I look for?
➤ What are the best methods to use when comparing poems?

## A comparison of themes

Table 3 suggests some ways in which the themes of all the poems you have studied could be compared. It does not cover every single point that could be compared, but it does give you an idea of how to group various poems and begin to work out the similarities and differences between them.

You may wish to develop the table: copy it out and add extra columns, or add more detailed cross-references.

## How to compare poems

It can be daunting to be asked to compare poems, especially as each poem was written to be read on its own and not to be analysed in an examination. However, it is not too hard if you approach the poems with the right questions. You will be asked to compare four poems. For each one, ask yourself:

* What is the **subject matter**? What is the story of the poem? What is it about?
* Whose **viewpoint** do we see things from? Is it in the first person or third person? If the first person, is it the poet talking, or have they taken on a persona?
* What is the **main theme**, or is there more than one main theme? What are the main ideas that the poet wants to explore? Look at Table 3 to help you.
* How does the poet **convey their message**? What are the key **images** and/or the main **features** of the poem? What **techniques** does the poet use? Look back at the notes on 'Structure', 'Language' and 'Imagery' in this book.

Table 3 Comparing techniques (continues on next page)

| | Nature | Water | Looking back; then and now | Family; parent/ child | Love, relation- ships, friendship | Death | Conflict |
|---|---|---|---|---|---|---|---|
| **Heaney** | | | | | | | |
| 'Storm on the Island' | ✓ | ✓ | | | | | ✓ |
| 'Perch' | ✓ | ✓ | ✓ | | | | |
| 'Blackberry-Picking' | ✓ | | ✓ | | ✓ | | |
| 'Death of a Naturalist' | ✓ | | ✓ | | | | ✓ |
| 'Digging' | ✓ | | ✓ | ✓ | | | |
| 'Mid-Term Break' | | | ✓ | | | ✓ | |
| 'Follower' | ✓ | | ✓ | ✓ | | | |
| 'At a Potato Digging' | ✓ | | ✓ | | | ✓ | |
| **Clarke** | | | | | | | |
| 'Catrin' | | | ✓ | ✓ | | | ✓ |
| 'Baby-sitting' | | | ✓ | ✓ | | | ✓ |
| 'Mali' | ✓ | ✓ | ✓ | ✓ | | | |
| 'A Difficult Birth, Easter 1998' | ✓ | | | | (✓) | | (✓) |
| 'The Field-Mouse' | ✓ | | | ✓ | | ✓ | ✓ |
| 'October' | ✓ | | | | ✓ | ✓ | |
| 'On the Train' | | | | ✓ | | ✓ | |
| 'Cold Knap Lake' | ✓ | ✓ | ✓ | ✓ | | ✓ | |

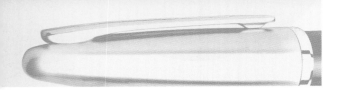

| | Nature | Water | Looking back; then and now | Family; parent/ child | Love, relation- ships, friendship | Death | Conflict |
|---|---|---|---|---|---|---|---|
| **Pre-1914 Poetry Bank** | | | | | | | |
| 'On my first Sonne' | | | | ✓ | | ✓ | |
| 'The Song of the Old Mother' | | | | ✓ | ✓ | | |
| 'The Affliction of Margaret' | | | ✓ | ✓ | | ✓ | |
| 'The Little Boy Lost/ Found' | (✓) | | | ✓ | ✓ | | |
| 'Tichborne's Elegy' | ✓ | | ✓ | | | | (✓) |
| 'The Man He Killed' | | | ✓ | | ✓ | ✓ | ✓ |
| 'Patrolling Barnegat' | ✓ | ✓ | | | | | ✓ |
| 'Sonnet 130' | | | | | ✓ | | |
| 'My Last Duchess' | | | ✓ | | ✓ | ✓ | ✓ |
| 'The Laboratory' | | | | | ✓ | ✓ | ✓ |
| 'Ulysses' | | ✓ | ✓ | ✓ | | ✓ | ✓ |
| 'The Village Schoolmaster' | | | ✓ | | ✓ | | |
| 'The Eagle' | ✓ | ✓ | | | | | (✓) |
| 'Inversnaid' | ✓ | ✓ | | | ✓ | | |
| 'Sonnet' | ✓ | ✓ | | | ✓ | | |

- What is the **tone** or **mood**? Think about how the poem should be read aloud — perhaps joyfully? Mournfully? Fearfully? With admiration? Lovingly? Angrily? Look back at the notes on 'Ideas to consider' in this book.
- What is your **own response**? Do you like the poem? Try to give a reason for your answer. What does it make you think of? What strikes you most about it? Look back at the 'Ideas to consider' in this book.

Perhaps the easiest way to approach comparative questions is to begin by making a table — then you can see if you have missed anything out. Let's say you want to look at four poems to **explore the relationship between parents and children**. You might choose 'Follower', 'Catrin', 'On my first Sonne' and 'The Little Boy Lost/Found'. You could begin by producing something like Table 4. Of course, this could be extended for other poems that include the relationship between parents and children, or you could make similar tables for the other themes.

Table 4 Comparing poems

| | 'Follower' | 'Catrin' | 'On My First Sonne' | 'The Little Boy Lost/Found' |
|---|---|---|---|---|
| **Subject matter** | Young Heaney follows his father ploughing; now his elderly father follows him | Clarke gives birth to her first child — the start of a lifetime of 'love and conflict' | Jonson mourns the death of his seven-year-old son | A young boy loses his father but is found by his mother — with the help of God |
| **Viewpoint** | Heaney as an adult looking back on his childhood | Clarke's, the mother's | Jonson's — a grieving parent | An omniscient observer (one who knows everything) |
| **Theme(s)** | Nature; looking back; parents and children | Parents and children; conflict; looking back | Parents and children; death | Parents and children; relationships (and nature, as it is set in a 'mire' and a 'lonely' fen) |
| **Style: structure, language and imagery** | Father as an expert — technical language; nautical imagery | Two stanzas represent past and present. 'Tight red rope of love' — love and conflict | Banking imagery: Jonson pays back God what is owed. Rhyming couplets | Sounds like a nursery rhyme — simple structure. God's role is unclear — sense of mystery |
| **Ideas to consider: tone/mood** | Affectionate, proud, wistful; now feels guilty? | Affectionate yet aware of tension | Heartfelt yet restrained | Sad and mournful when the child is lost; relieved and joyful when he's found |
| **Ideas to consider: your response** | Beautiful picture of rural childhood | Honest. Shows the difficulty in letting go | Brave: Jonson tries to persuade himself his son is now better off | Puzzling. What is significance of the 'vapour' and 'wand'ring light'? |

Alternatively, you could make structured notes on each poem in turn. If, for example, you are asked to **compare the portrayal of water** in four poems, you might select 'Patrolling Barnegat', 'Cold Knap Lake', 'Inversnaid', and 'Perch', and jot down ideas like this:

'Patrolling Barnegat': water is wild and dangerous. First-person narrator sees water as wild, powerful, out of control: perhaps causes a wreck, part of 'savage trinity'. '–ing' rhymes suggest incessant and constant action. Shows raw energy of nature.

'Cold Knap Lake': water is calm yet still dangerous. Child almost drowns —caused by weed, 'water's long green silk' — but is rescued by poet's mother. Water then seen as mysterious, possibly hiding something 'shadowy' and, strangely, covering 'All lost things'. Fairy tale?

'Inversnaid': water is at times dangerous but also vital for life. Poet shows us a 'pitchblack' whirlpool — possibly so dangerous it drowns 'Despair' itself. Yet poet also shows us water as energetic and lively, 'roaring' down a waterfall to a lake. Burn is personified — it 'treads through' landscape, as if being careful. Poem ends with plea to conserve the 'wildness and wet' in the world — shows water's value.

'Perch': water is home for the fish — sanctuary. Poet refers to 'the river's glorified body' and 'carpets of Bann stream'. He is praising the water as well as the perch. Fish rely on the water: it provides their food — 'Guzzling the current'. Playful tone.

When you have jotted down notes, practise writing a few paragraphs outlining the comparisons you wish to make. Here are two paragraphs comparing four poems on the **theme of conflict**. The poems chosen were 'The Man He Killed', 'The Field-Mouse', 'My Last Duchess' and 'Death of a Naturalist'.

Hardy and Clarke are both writing about conflict on a grand scale, wars between nations. Both convey the human cost of war. Hardy does this through describing the man he killed as someone 'just as I', 'a fellow' whom in other circumstances he'd 'treat if met where any bar is'. Clarke shows the bloody reality by examining the gory death of a single field-mouse during an afternoon's haymaking and projecting its 'agony big as itself' onto the scene in 'Europe', where 'the air [is] stammering with gunfire'.

Browning and Heaney, however, look at conflict on a more personal level. The Duke of Ferrara admits to being in conflict with his wife over her behaviour towards other men — 'She had/A heart — how shall I say? — too soon made glad' and he hints that he took action to prevent it: 'I gave commands; Then all smiles stopped together.' He does not appear to feel guilty for ending the conflict between them in the most violent way possible. In contrast to the persona Browning adopts in 'My Last Duchess', the speaker in 'Death of a Naturalist' is the poet himself, and he is arguably not the perpetrator of the conflict but the victim. The 'angry frogs' wanted 'vengeance' and they 'sat/Poised like mud grenades' as if ready to attack the young Heaney.

It would be useful to practise writing similar paragraphs using four poems linked by other themes. The more connections and links between the poems you record, the easier it will be to choose poems that suit the question posed in the exam.

Remember, however, that not all questions in the exam will necessarily be theme-based. You might also be asked to look at four poems written in the first person, or four poems that use rhyme effectively. These paragraphs are about four poems written to *convey the poet's own feelings*: Clare's 'Sonnet', 'Tichborne's Elegy', 'Digging' and 'October'.

'Tichborne's Elegy' and 'October' are both highly personal poems about death. Tichborne was in the awful situation of contemplating his own death, which was to take place the following day. In his poem, he laments the waste of potential by using metaphors in balanced lines to show the contrast between how things are for him and how he wishes they would be: 'My feast of joy is but a dish of pain; My crop of corn is but a field of tares'. Interestingly, Clarke laments the fact that she does not know when her death will be. Having mourned the death of her friend, she goes on to feel 'panic' that she passes her own 'death-day' every year without realising it, and this inspires her to 'write like the wind', 'winning ground'.

In contrast to these sad, contemplative poems, Heaney uses 'Digging' to show his affection for and pride in his father and grandfather: 'By God, the old man could handle a spade. Just like his old man.' He has a need to follow in the family tradition: he decides he will 'dig' with his pen. He uses the poem to express the idea that writing about members of his family is a way of following in their footsteps.

A less introspective poem, Clare's 'Sonnet' is a simple expression of personal joy at a beautiful view. He repeats 'I love to see', emphasising the pleasure he gains from looking at a peaceful, natural scene. He takes time to point out even the smallest elements — 'bright beetles in the clear lake play' — that have a part in the 'beaming' summer's day.

You could use Table 2 on pages 82–83, which summarises poetic techniques, to practise linking other poems in this way.

There are also some sample exam questions in the section on 'Tackling the exam' (pages 96–98) that you can use to practise with.

# Tackling the exam

As you read this section, ask yourself:
➤ Which grade are you aiming for?
➤ Which exam skills do you need to practise?
➤ How can you be sure you do what's needed on the day to gain your target grade?

The poetry question is worth a full **40%** of your entire English literature grade, so it is important to write the best answer you can to impress the examiners.

Let's remind ourselves of the **Assessment Objectives** (AO) for the English literature examination — in other words, what the examiners are looking for and what they are able to give marks for. Candidates are asked to:

* AO1: respond to texts critically, sensitively and in detail, selecting appropriate ways to convey their response, using textual evidence as appropriate.
* AO2: explore how language, structure and forms contribute to the meanings of texts, considering different approaches to texts and alternative interpretations.
* AO3: explore relationships and comparisons between texts, selecting and evaluating relevant material.

## Key point

The Assessment Objectives are *equally weighted*, so you have to respond to each one to get a good grade. You are advised to spend roughly the same amount of time preparing for each Assessment Objective to be tested. In the past, some able candidates have let themselves down by ignoring one of the Assessment Objectives. However good your writing, you will not earn top marks if you don't discuss the poets' methods or you don't compare the poems!

# Examination tips: how to get a top mark

## Timing

Remember that you have just 1 hour and 45 minutes to complete both parts of the written paper. The exam board suggests you spend 45 minutes on Section A (prose text) and **1 hour on the poetry question**. You might want to do the poetry section first, when you are fresher, but do remember to allow yourself long enough for the prose question too: writing a fantastic answer on poetry but nothing on prose will lose you valuable marks.

Plan your hour carefully. You should spend:

- 5 minutes choosing which question to answer
- 10 minutes planning your answer
- 40 minutes writing
- 5 minutes checking your work

## Read the questions carefully

The examiners try to set a range of questions that allow you to write about whatever poems you feel comfortable with, so read all the questions carefully to ensure that you spend your hour answering the question that is right for you. Don't leap into the first question on the paper, or a question that happens to feature your favourite poem without considering how you would link it to three other poems. When you have decided, write the number of the question in the box on the front of your answer paper, so that the examiner knows immediately what to expect.

## Planning your answer

- Use a highlighter pen to highlight key words or phrases in the poem, so that you know what you are focusing on. As you are planning and writing, refer back frequently to make sure that you are actually answering the question.
- There is *no* requirement for balance. In other words, you do not have to write exactly the same amount on each of the four poems. However, you do need to show a good knowledge of each poem, so it is best to write *similar* amounts on each one. (Writing four pages on two poems and only half a page on the other two is unlikely to show your full appreciation of the poems' meanings and ideas.)
- Remember that if a question is presented in two parts, it is important to devote equal weight to both parts. You can, if you wish, write a two-part essay for a two-part question (unless the wording of the question makes clear that you should write an integrated essay).
- For each poem, try to comment on each of the aspects discussed earlier in this book (see Table 4 on page 89). You need to consider what the poets wanted to say and how they said it, so jot down the main points on:
  - subject matter

* viewpoint
* themes
* structure, language and imagery
* ideas to consider — mood or tone
* ideas to consider — your response

Then work out how you will include these points in your essay.

## Choosing your language

You will impress the examiner by the elegance of your writing and the way in which you present your ideas. Guide the reader through your writing with phrases like those below. All of the following examples could come from an essay comparing the attitudes of the Duke of Ferrara ('My Last Duchess', Browning) and Ulysses ('Ulysses', Tennyson) towards other people. You can vary the phrases to suit any essay you are writing. Key phrases are in italic and those particular to the examples being discussed are in normal type.

### Introductory phrases

* *Perhaps the most striking thing about these poems* is that both men are clearly powerful rulers, *yet both poets allow us to explore* why it is that the Duke and Ulysses act as they do.
* *One theme that unites these poems is* reflection: both men look back to events in the past.
* *It may be because these poems were written* only three *years apart that* they share many ideas and themes.
* *On first reading, the two poems seem very similar because* both feature powerful men who have control over life and death. *However*, it becomes apparent that the Duke wields this power for selfish reasons, while Ulysses is arguably less selfish, hoping to do 'Some work of noble note'.
* *When I first read* 'Ulysses' *I was puzzled that* the hero could leave his country with his son in charge, *but* when I read 'My Last Duchess' I realised that this is preferable to being ruled over by a tyrant.

### Comparing similar features

* *Both poems are written* in the first person: Browning and Tennyson bring the characters to life by taking on their personas.
* *The effective use of* the iambic pentameter in 'Ulysses' *also features in* 'My Last Duchess', to give the impression of the patterns of natural speech.
* 'Ulysses' *includes an idea also contained in* 'My Last Duchess': neither the Duke nor Ulysses is attached to their wives.
* *Like* 'My Last Duchess', 'Ulysses' ends on an intriguing note: we don't know whether the Duke will obtain his 'fair' new wife or whether Ulysses' mission 'to seek, to find' will succeed.

- *I feel the two poems are alike because* of the strong image that is portrayed not only of both men but of their motives.

### Contrasting different features

- *While* the Duke *refers to* the recent past, Ulysses concentrates on his memories of further back — the great successes of his youth.
- *However*, Ulysses' friendly relationship with his servants *is different* to the Duke's commanding attitude.
- *Unlike* 'Ulysses', *which is written in* blank verse, 'My Last Duchess' is composed of rhyming couplets — although they are not immediately obvious as they are not all end-stopped.
- *I feel the two poems are different because of* the scale of their subjects. 'My Last Duchess' is, arguably, little more than the tale of a jealous husband, while 'Ulysses' takes on a grander perspective.
- *The main contrast between* 'Ulysses' *and* 'My Last Duchess' *is* that Ulysses is a sympathetic hero (whom we can admire even if we do not agree with his actions), *while* the Duke is certainly a villain.
- *Although it could be said* that we learn more about the other characters in 'My Last Duchess' (including the Duchess herself and Frà Pandolf), *I think that* Ulysses' praise of his son Telemachus is important.

### Concluding phrases

- *In conclusion, both poems* provide a dramatic illustration of how powerful men may treat other people.
- *From exploring the poems carefully, it seems that* both the Duke and Ulysses are well practised in dealing with other people. Both have found ways of treating their family and servants to achieve their own goals.
- *What I will remember about these poems is* the vivid portrayals of two strong leaders.

## Back up your points

It is crucial that you refer to the poems in detail throughout your essay. The examiner will, of course, know all the poems well — but you still need to use quotations to prove the points you are making. A good way to remember this is to PEE on your work: make a <u>P</u>oint, provide the <u>E</u>vidence (a quotation) and <u>E</u>xplain why the quotation is relevant. The quotations should be brief and pithy. Here's an example from an essay. The point is in blue, the evidence is in orange and the explanation is in green.

### Key point

Gillian Clarke gives some tips to exam success on her website, including:
- ➤ Remember, in a poem every word counts.
- ➤ Bring your experience, your heart and mind to the poem.
- ➤ Trust the images that come into your mind.

The Duke is a harsh man, used to being in control. He chooses 'Never to stoop', which suggests he enjoys being dominant over others, particularly those he sees as of a lower status. Ulysses, however, treats his sailors more humanely. He refers to them as 'Souls that have toiled, and wrought, and thought with me', which implies that he sees them as his equals and respects them.

Don't just list features in a poem. You'll get no marks for pointing out a simile, but you'll get lots if you explain *how* it contributes to the poem.

## Spelling and punctuation

A maximum of three marks will be given for accuracy — so it really is worth reading your work through carefully when you have finished writing to check that it makes sense. It could make the difference between a good grade and a great grade.

# Practice questions

Higher-tier and foundation-tier questions are very similar. The key difference is that foundation-tier questions include more guidance and tips; higher-tier candidates have to brainstorm the hints for themselves.

Have a go at these sample questions. Plan your answers as if you were about to tackle each question in the examination.

## Higher tier

1  (a) 'Compare Ben Jonson's presentation of his feelings in 'On my first Sonne' with the way in which William Wordsworth presents feelings in 'The Affliction of Margaret'.

(b) Then compare these two poems with two of the following poems:
'Digging' (Seamus Heaney)
'Mid-Term Break' (Seamus Heaney)
'Follower' (Seamus Heaney)
'The Field-Mouse' (Gillian Clarke)
'On the Train' (Gillian Clarke)
'Cold Knap Lake' (Gillian Clarke)

2  Death is a theme shared by many poems in your *Anthology*.

(a) Choose either 'Mid-Term Break' or 'At a Potato Digging' by Seamus Heaney and compare the poet's attitude to death and how death is presented with either 'The Field-Mouse' or 'On the Train' by Gillian Clarke.

(b) Consider 'The Eagle' by Tennyson and one other poem from the Pre-1914 Poetry Bank about death; compare and contrast the poets' attitudes to death and how they present this theme.

3 'People work in harmony with nature.'
  (a) Choose one poem by Seamus Heaney and one poem by Gillian Clarke that you could use either to support or contradict this statement.
  (b) Choose two poems from the Pre-1914 Poetry Bank, one of which could be used to support the statement and one of which could be used as evidence against it. Explain your choices through close reference to both poems.

4 (a) Compare the ways in which Gillian Clarke presents relationships between people in 'Catrin' and one other of her poems.
  (b) Choose two poems from the Pre-1914 Poetry Bank that also feature human relationships. What do you find similar and different in the ways that these relationships are portrayed?

## Foundation tier

1 (a) Many of the poems show us the poets' feelings and emotions. Compare Ben Jonson's presentation of his feelings of loss in 'On my first Sonne' with the way in which William Wordsworth presents feelings of loss in 'The Affliction of Margaret'.
  (b) Then compare each of these poems with one of the following poems:
    'Digging' (Seamus Heaney)
    'Mid-Term Break' (Seamus Heaney)
    'Follower' (Seamus Heaney)
    'The Field-Mouse' (Gillian Clarke)
    'On the Train' (Gillian Clarke)
    'Cold Knap Lake' (Gillian Clarke)

2 Death is a theme shared by many poems in your *Anthology*.
  (a) Choose either 'Mid-Term Break' or 'At a Potato Digging' by Seamus Heaney to compare with either 'The Field-Mouse' or 'On the Train' by Gillian Clarke.
    ✳ How do each of the poets present death?
    ✳ What do they feel about the deaths they describe?
  (b) Consider 'The Eagle' by Tennyson and choose one other poem from the Pre-1914 Poetry Bank about death.
    ✳ Compare the ways in which the two poets present death.
    ✳ How do they feel about the deaths they describe?

3 'People work in harmony with nature.'
  (a) To what extent do you agree with this statement? Choose one poem by Seamus Heaney and one poem by Gillian Clarke that either supports or contradicts the statement.

(b) Choose two poems from the Pre-1914 Poetry Bank, one of which could be used to support the statement and one of which could be used as evidence against it. In each case, explain your choices through close reference to both poems. Remember to comment on:

* the language and imagery used by the poets to describe our relationship with nature
* their attitude towards our relationship with nature

4 (a) Compare the ways in which Gillian Clarke presents the relationship between herself and her daughter in 'Catrin' and the parent/child relationship in one other of her poems.

(b) Choose two poems from the Pre-1914 Poetry Bank that also feature human relationships. These can be parent/child relationships, or the relationship between lovers (or a husband and wife), or between masters and servants.

* What do you find similar in the ways that these relationships are portrayed?
* What do you find different?

# What does it take to get an A grade?

The criteria that the examiners use to mark your essays are carefully designed to help you get the best mark of which you are capable. Examiners mark what you have written and not what you *haven't* written (or, in other words, you won't lose marks if you miss out a couple of points). So it's up to you to write about the poems in as much significant detail as possible. You can see from the grade guidelines below what it takes to earn a top mark.

Grade A Candidates respond critically and sensitively to the poems, taking into account alternative approaches and interpretations. They explore and evaluate the ways meanings, ideas and feelings are conveyed through language, structure and form, making connections and comparisons between them.

Grade C In responding to poems, candidates show understanding of how meanings and ideas are conveyed through language, structure and form. They explore connections and comparisons between the poems, referring to details to support their views.

Grade F In giving personal responses to poems, candidates show understanding of key features, including themes and language. They make straightforward connections between the poems, and refer to aspects of texts when explaining their views.

# Sample answer

Here is a sample answer to higher-tier question 1. It would earn an A* grade.

**1 (a) Compare Ben Jonson's presentation of his feelings in 'On my first Sonne' with the way in which William Wordsworth presents feelings in 'The Affliction of Margaret'.**

Introduction: subject matter and viewpoint

Both poems portray a parent's sorrow at the loss of a son. Jonson's son has died, aged only seven years old, and Jonson, in his grief, writes a very personal poem, perhaps to try to convince himself that death really is the best thing for the boy. Margaret, on the other hand, is a fictional creation. Wordsworth has created a persona of a woman whose son has disappeared — she does not know whether he is dead, but fears the worst.

Language: to whom poems are addressed. Comparison

Both poems are addressed directly to the lost children. Jonson's approach is gentle, 'Farewell', as if his son is departing on a journey. It is not immediately obvious to the reader that he has died. Indeed, Jonson speaks throughout as if the child can hear him, which perhaps suggests an inability to accept that the boy is dead.

Example of: point evidence explanation

Margaret's appeal is more direct, with the repetition of 'Where art thou' indicating her desperation for news. For Margaret, the fact that she does not know whether her son lives or not is 'worse to me than dead'. She is in limbo — she may feel that if she had proof of his death she could mourn properly and move on.

Tone, mood

Discusses imagery

Jonson's poem is brief and restrained. The six pairs of rhyming couplets contain poignant imagery. Jonson sees his son as having been 'lent' to him by God and accepts that the time came, 'the just day', for the debt to be repaid. It may seem callous to a modern reader that human lives can be compared to financial transactions, but here it shows Jonson's unquestioning faith in God. It was God who allowed him to have the child in the first place; the boy will lie with God in 'soft peace'.

Contrast: tone, mood

Note that quotations are embedded throughout

Wordsworth's poem, on the other hand, is longer and, despite the strict structure of the stanzas, appears more rambling. This reflects Margaret's troubled mind and suggests that she has long dwelt on her troubles. She remembers her son when he was a child, 'beauteous to behold', and torments herself by wondering what may have happened to him. She has rejected the idea that he has neglected her, so is he impoverished, imprisoned or dead? The fact that 'The very shadows of the clouds' disturb her shows the extent of her suffering.

Perhaps the most thought-provoking part of each poem is the
ending. Having experienced the loss of what he treasured most,
Jonson vows never again to love anything 'too much'. We feel he
could not bear to go through the same anguish again. Margaret's
anguish is stated more clearly: she is 'beyond relief' and has 'no
other earthly friend'. We may sympathise with them both.

**(b) Then compare these two poems with two of the following poems:**
   **'Digging' (Seamus Heaney)**
   **'Mid-Term Break' (Seamus Heaney)**
   **'Follower' (Seamus Heaney)**
   **'The Field-Mouse' (Gillian Clarke)**
   **'On the Train' (Gillian Clarke)**
   **'Cold Knap Lake' (Gillian Clarke)**

I have chosen to focus on 'Mid-Term Break' and 'On the Train'
because both poems, like Jonson's and Wordsworth's, are
concerned with an individual's reactions to death.

'Mid-Term Break' is very similar to 'On my first Sonne', in that both
are written in the first person and both express great pain in a
controlled yet moving way. Whereas Jonson chooses a pun to
portray his love of and pride in his son ('his best piece of poetrie'),
Heaney uses simple images to convey his emotions on the death

of his younger brother. In the personification of 'Snowdrops/And
candles soothed the bedside', we see how the pure, white flowers
and the candles that remind us of light and hope actually soothed
Heaney. Even the cause of the child's death, an impact 'on his left
temple', is described in picturesque terms, 'a poppy bruise':

Heaney's last memory of his brother is one of beauty and peace.

'Mid-Term Break' also explores the emotions experienced by other
people. Heaney tells us of his 'father crying' — his father being a
man who never cried — and of the 'angry tearless sighs' his mother
'coughed out'. Although 'The Affliction of Margaret' deals solely
with one woman's grief, here too we see different types of emotion
expressed, probably because Margaret has suffered for so many
years. Sometimes she feels she is in 'darkness', at others she
'[wept] for him when no one knew', at others she 'look[ed] for
Ghosts'. It is interesting that neither Margaret nor Heaney take
comfort from God (despite the 'knelling' bells and 'candles' that
remind us of Heaney's Catholic background), when it is this that
gives relief to Jonson.

Comparison:
subject matter
and imagery

Tone, mood

'On the Train' is the only poem not to describe the loss of someone close to the speaker. Gillian Clarke writes of the deaths of strangers killed in a train crash. She describes the horror of how those 'Cradled' on a train all at once became passengers on a 'blazing bone-ship', a graphic image that suggests sacrificial death. Presenting us with the sound of answer-phone messages on mobile phones that will never be answered again, she goes on to express her desire to contact her own loved ones: 'talk to me, please. Pick up the phone.' The repeated request shows her urgent need for reassurance. These deaths, then, prompt in the poet emotions of shock and sympathy for the victims and an impulse to connect to the living. Because she is not related to any of the dead, her feelings are different to those expressed by Jonson, Margaret and Heaney.

Conclusion: refers
back to the question;
personal response

The four poems all display personal feelings that arise through experiencing the death (or probable death, in Margaret's case) of other human beings. As such, they reflect the multitude of emotions that we all may experience. I was most struck by the pared-down, disciplined yet profound grief expressed by Jonson and Heaney, perhaps best illustrated by Heaney's haunting concluding line: 'A four foot box, a foot for every year.'

# Answers

Answers to 'Review your learning' questions.

## Context (page 10)

1 Clarke
2 Heaney
3 Heaney
4 Clarke

## Themes (page 76)

1 Ireland, his childhood, his family, nature as an ally, nature as an enemy
2 her family and motherhood, nature, death, reactions to outside events
3 war
4 the future

## Style (page 85)

1 false
2 true
3 true
4 false
5 true

# Glossary of literary terms

**alliteration** The repetition of the first letter or sound of nearby words to create an effect. The strong alliteration in this example suggests the power of the eagle: 'He clasps the crag with crooked hands' ('The Eagle', Tennyson).

**ambiguous** This describes a word or phrase that has more than one meaning, or could be read in two ways. The description of the Duchess's death in 'My Last Duchess' is ambiguous: 'I gave commands;/Then all smiles stopped together.' We are not exactly certain *how* the 'smiles stopped', but we feel sure the Duke killed her.

**assonance** The repetition of a vowel sound (or a similar vowel sound) in nearby words to create an effect. In this example the assonance on the long vowels 'o' and 'a' suggests the lengthy wait: 'The long day wanes: the slow moon climbs' ('Ulysses', Tennyson).

**blank verse** Lines of unrhymed iambic pentameter verse, such as Browning's 'My Last Duchess'. It is a traditional style in English literature; Shakespeare's plays are in blank verse.

**caesura** A break mid-way through a line of poetry, often to give a sense of balance, as in 'Tichborne's Elegy':

> My tale was heard,/and yet it was not told,
> My fruit is fallen,/and yet my leaves are green.

**consonance** The repetition of consonants within nearby words to create an effect. In this example, consonance combines with alliteration to show the rush of the water: 'His rollrock highroad roaring down' ('Inversnaid', Hopkins).

**dramatic monologue** A long poem in which one speaker addresses an imaginary audience, such as Tennyson's 'Ulysses'.

**elegy** A poem of mourning or lamentation for the dead, such as Jonson's 'On my first Sonne'.

**end-stopped** Finishing with a full stop or other punctuation to mark a pause at the end of a line of poetry. This example is from Goldsmith's 'The Village Schoolmaster':

> There, in his noisy mansion, skilled to rule,
> The village master taught his little school

**enjambement** Lines of poetry that are not end-stopped, but where the sense flows into the following line, are said to be enjambed. This device can be used to make blank verse sound natural, and to create other effects. Hopkins uses it in 'Inversnaid' to suggest the constant flow of water: '...the fleece of his foam/Flutes and...'.

**euphemism** A phrase that attempts to avoid embarrassment or unpleasantness. For example, 'passed over' is a euphemism for 'died'.

**first person** Written from the writer's point of view. 'I' is used: 'I think my love as rare' ('Sonnet 130', Shakespeare).

**iambic pentameter** An iamb is a metrical foot of one unstressed syllable followed by a stressed one, such as 'I <u>do</u>'. Five iambs in a row make an iambic pentameter. This is a perfect example: 'To <u>strive</u>, to <u>seek</u>, to <u>find</u> and <u>not</u> to <u>yield</u>' ('Ulysses', Tennyson).

**irony** Occurs in an expression that has two meanings — an obvious one, and an 'inner', possibly sarcastic, meaning for those in the know. Goldsmith used irony in 'The Village Schoolmaster': 'Twas certain he could write, and cipher too'. On the surface he is praising the skills of the schoolmaster, but we realise it is only faint praise — of course a schoolmaster should be able to write and do arithmetic!

**metaphor** An image that suggests that one thing is something else as a way of comparing them. Clare describes 'clouds sailing to the north' as if they were ships ('Sonnet'), to help us imagine them scudding through the sky. **Extended metaphor** is a metaphor that continues over a number of lines or even the whole poem, such as the image of Heaney's father ploughing being a ship in full sail ('Follower').

**onomatopoeia** A word that sounds like the item it refers to, like 'buzz' or 'whoosh'. Heaney describes spray that 'spits' ('Storm on the Island') and Clarke writes 'The air hums with jets' ('The Field-Mouse').

**oxymoron** A contradictory phrase that sounds impossible on first hearing but which actually contains some truth, such as 'inhuman men' ('The Affliction of Margaret', Wordsworth).

**pentameter** See **iambic pentameter**.

**persona** A role taken on by a writer. The writer pretends to be someone else and writes from that person's point of view. Examples include Wordsworth in 'The Affliction of Margaret' and Browning in 'The Laboratory'.

**personification** Talking about an object or an animal as if it were a human to create an effect, as in: 'Till stars are beginning to blink and peep' ('The Song of the Old Mother', Yeats).

**pronouns** Words like *it*, *its*, *they* used to avoid repeating the name of an object or objects. **Personal pronouns** are words like *I*, *you*, *he*, *she* used to avoid repeating the name of a person or people.

**pun** A play on words, such as 'In the finland of perch': here, the poet reminds us that perch have fins and Finland is a country ('Perch', Heaney).

**quatrain** A stanza of poetry that is four lines long. Browning's 'The Laboratory' is made up of 12 quatrains.

**refrain** A line (or lines) that recurs at the end of stanzas in a poem, such as 'And now I live, and now my life is done' in 'Tichborne's Elegy'.

**rhetorical question** A question that is asked for effect, without an answer really being expected: 'What would the world be, once bereft/Of wet and of wildness?' ('Inversnaid', Hopkins).

**rhyme** The repetition of the same sound at the end of nearby lines of poetry, such as 'wet'/'met' and 'face'/'place' in 'The Man He Killed' by Thomas Hardy. **Half-rhyme** is near rhyme, such as 'ready'/'body' and 'slur'/'air' in Heaney's 'Perch'.

**Rhyming couplets** are pairs of iambic rhyming lines, such as the conclusion to Shakespeare's 'Sonnet 130': 'And yet, by heaven, I think my love as rare/As any she belied with false compare.' **Heroic couplets** are long series of rhyming couplets, often used in dramatic monologues, so called because they were used by ancient Greek poets when writing heroic tales of battle.

**simile** An image that compares one thing to another using 'like' or 'as'. In 'like a thunderbolt he falls' ('The Eagle', Tennyson), we appreciate the sudden speed and immense strength of the bird.

**tenses** **Past tense** is used for what has already happened: 'she smiled, no doubt, /Whene'er I passed her'. **Present tense** refers to what is happening now: 'I call/That piece a wonder'. **Future tense** describes what will happen: 'we'll go/Together down, sir.' (All these examples are taken from Browning's 'My Last Duchess'.)